e Little Class with the Big Personality

of related interest

Snapshots of Autism
A Family Album
Jennifer Overton
ISBN 1 84310 723 6

I'm not Naughty – I'm Autistic
Jodi's Journey
Jean Shaw
ISBN 1 84310 105 X

Running with Walker
A Memoir
Robert Hughes
ISBN 1 84310 755 4

Multicoloured Mayhem
Parenting the many shades of adolescents and children with autism,
Asperger Syndrome and AD/HD
Jacqui Jackson
ISBN 1 84310 171 8

Parent to Parent
Information and Inspiration for Parents Dealing
with Autism or Asperger's Syndrome
Ann Boushéy
ISBN 1 84310 774 0

How to Live with Autism and Asperger Syndrome
Practical Strategies for Parents and Professionals
Christine Williams and Barry Wright
Illustrated by Olive Young
ISBN 1 84310 184 X

How To Understand Autism – The Easy Way
Alex Durig
ISBN 1 84310 791 0

The Little Class with the Big Personality

Experiences of Teaching a Class of Young Children with Autism

Fran Hunnisett

Jessica Kingsley Publishers
London and Philadelphia

First published in 2005
by Jessica Kingsley Publishers
116 Pentonville Road
London N1 9JB, UK
and
400 Market Street, Suite 400
Philadelphia, PA 19106, USA

www.jkp.com

Copyright © Fran Hunnisett 2005

Library of Congress Cataloging in Publication Data
A CIP catalog record for this book is available from the Library of Congress

British Library Cataloguing in Publication Data
A CIP catalogue record for this book is available from the British Library

ISBN-13: 978 1 84310 308 0
ISBN-10: 1 84310 308 7

Printed and bound in Great Britain by
Athenaeum Press, Gateshead, Tyne and Wear

No man's knowledge
can go beyond his experience.

John Locke

'But we don't want to teach 'em' replied the
Badger. 'We want to learn 'em...'

Kenneth Grahame,
The Wind in the Willows

Acknowledgements

A huge 'thank you' to the seven children who inspired me to write this book. Their determination, humour and BIG personalities have enriched my life and given me much happiness.

Thanks also to their parents. Their constant good humour and generosity have helped me far more than they realise and I want to thank them for their trust and friendship over the years.

I am indebted to Janice for her expertise, advice and technological support and for spurring me on to 'go public' with the book, and to Elaine – for reading (and enjoying) the manuscript and correcting my mistakes!

Extended thanks also go to the staff at the Unit, both past and present, but especially all those I worked closely with over the years.

Finally thanks to my parents for being proud of me and my family for – well, all sorts, really!

Contents

Preface

The events described in this book took place at a school in the north of England for children with autism. When the author joined the school it was known as 'the Unit' for reasons more to do with lack of imagination than informative titles. Gradually, as the status and size of the Unit increased, that title became meaningless. The establishment now has a respectable, grown-up school name and many more pupils. Although most parents refer to the school by name, in the book I have used the term 'the Unit' as a way of protecting the anonymity of the school.

The pupils still attend this now grown-up school, and are themselves growing into young adults. They are no longer all in the same class, but their parents keep in touch and that sense of community that developed in those early years is still strong. When I first made my rather tentative approaches to the parents about writing a book about my first three years as a teacher at the Unit I was not sure what their reactions might be. They were unanimously enthusiastic about the project and gave me all the help I could have asked for.

We reminisced about the variety of emotions, experiences and challenges that made up those early years of their sons' and daughters' education. The interviews in this book are wonderfully honest accounts of how it feels to be a mother or a father of a child with autism handing over the care of your child, albeit for only five short days a week, into the care of a stranger. Whilst talking to the parents it struck me that in those three years the foundations were laid for lasting friendships that continue to this day.

In these days of educational testing and target setting I think it is important not to lose sight of the real value of education. In the small community that made up my first class, we all, parents, children and teachers, shared in the learning process and I think we all took away some valuable lessons from the experience. Ultimately, though, the most influential teachers at that time were the children themselves. And they are still teaching us.

Alice's Illustrations

Alice, now in her teens, appeared matter of fact when I asked her if she would like to produce the illustrations for a book I was writing about her first class. Her approach to the task was methodical and thorough. As she got used to the idea, she began to relax and while she drew we reminisced about that first class. Sometimes, as she started a drawing, Alice would begin to chuckle. She wouldn't tell me who the drawing was about as she was working on it, but she let me see it in various stages of completion, inviting me to guess who it might be that she was drawing and what the theme of the picture was. It was not until she had finished the collection of drawings some weeks later that her look of disappointment confirmed what I had suspected. Alice had thoroughly enjoyed giving up her time to help me and would have happily continued forever if only I had needed her to. Her love of drawing had certainly not diminished since she was a little girl in Class One.

What has changed is her style. As she has grown up Alice, perhaps inevitably, has lost some of the spontaneity of her early years. If some of the children in the pictures look older than expected it is because Alice is now a young teenager. The rather glamorous girls and hunky boys in some of the drawings reflect her interests in American cartoons and computer games more than the memory of how her classmates looked when they were five and six years old.

Even so she remembers their spirit, and the subjects she has chosen to celebrate moments in that first class are very apt. A rather mature looking Lotti is floating in a pool, a wonderful reflection of her love of water. Sam is seen reluctantly being taken for a walk by his teacher (who looks remarkably like me, I must admit!). She has captured a typical pose of Nathan's, hunched up on a chair with his coat over his head. Like me, she remembers Liam's love of taped music and Joss's love of the train set that filled the quieter moments of his energetic early years. Toby on a spacehopper reminds us of his energy and bounce. Her picture of herself, with Toby, waltzing around the classroom is a fitting picture to represent a little girl who loved make-believe – the prince and princess in their briefly created make-believe world of fairy tales come true.

One week, at my home, she came across the naughty little princess from Tony Ross's book *I Want My Potty*. We recalled the fun times we had as a class shouting out 'She wants her potty!' and it was clear that, despite her love of more glamorous princesses, this scruffy 'teddy princess', as Alice calls her, holds a place of affection in Alice's memories just as it does in mine. She drew this picture of the little princess. I include it as a testimony to the fun we had as a class sharing, in our own unique ways, this much loved story. I'm sure Tony Ross would be pleased to know how his little princess has brought together a class of children with autism and their teachers, helping to bind them into a very special community and learning a little bit along the way about the true meaning of education.

Introduction

No Rainman

> You get the Autism Awareness week and you get all these marvellous autistic savants creeping out of the woodwork. It's annoying because the first thing you get is 'Oh, autistic! They're really clever aren't they?'
>
> You are like 'No!'
>
> 'You mean he can't count chopsticks thrown on the floor?'
>
> (Quote from parent, talking about the general perception of autism)

After a year of teaching a class of seven children with autism in a special school I realised that nothing in the reading I had absorbed, the programmes that I had watched or the conferences I had attended related completely to my own experience as a teacher of a vibrant class of five- to seven-year-olds. These children, despite all having a diagnosis of autism, were as individual, unique and overflowing with personality as any child I had taught in the busy mainstream schools that had informed my earlier career as a primary school teacher.

I was continually thirsty for knowledge about autism, eager for any insight into this complex condition. One day at school I was enthusing to Liam's parents about a programme I had seen the previous night. It was about Clara, a young woman with autism who was now making a living selling her paintings. Some years earlier I had read an account of the first eight years of Clara's life (Claiborne Park 1983). It detailed her journey through an array of fears and challenges to come to some understanding of how to function in an apparently frightening world. I had been very moved by the dedication, determination and hopefulness that surrounded this little girl who was frightened of the colour red and overwhelmed by her own identity.

Talking with Liam's parents about the programme and its optimistic outlook, I was brought up short by Warren's response. Without self-pity he said:

> That's all very well, Fran, but that's not our Liam. He's just an ordinary boy with autism and he always will be. He doesn't make a good story or interesting TV. There's going to be no miracle cure. He's just who he is with all his difficulties. No one wants to know about the ordinary ones.

Looking at Liam pacing the perimeter of the playground, head pressed against the metal structure, eyes fixed on the passing pattern of wire mesh, I knew what Warren meant. Liam was Liam, a boy with autism who would plod through life much like we all do, with no one to blow his trumpet for him and without the talents of a 'Rainman' to impress and intrigue the wider world. He was just an ordinary child from an ordinary family living with an extraordinary diagnosis and battling through life to make the best of it.

Except that he wasn't just ordinary, any more than any of the other seven children in my class of autistic children was simply ordinary. There was Joss, with his love of running; Alice, waiting to meet her Prince Charming; thoughtful Nathan and gregarious Toby; Lotti, with her love of wind and rain; peace-loving Sam and Liam – cheeky Liam with his capacity to liven up the whole class with one mischievous action. Each of these children brought something of themselves that profoundly changed my understanding of autism and affected me personally in a way I still find difficult to express. Each shared the same diagnosis – a diagnosis that suggested a standardised absence of character – yet each was so different from the other that their vibrant personalities were of far more significance in defining who they were than their shared diagnosis of autism.

It is these 'ordinary' children with autism who are the very ones we should be celebrating. These are the ones who should have a public voice because each one of them helps us see beyond stereotypes, labels, diagnosis and misconception to bring us back to the truth that we are all a part of this rich spectrum of humanity that makes up the human race.

It is all too easy to set children with autism up as rare creatures, both fascinating and intriguing. There is something about the condition that excites our curiosity. Autism has been referred to as an enigma and there are two commonly held but contrasting views about what it means to be autistic. One view is that everyone with autism has some wonderful, exotic talent that shines through their strangeness, so that we can marvel and shake our heads in wonder. The apparent redeeming factor of an extraordinary talent amidst an otherwise crippling condition somehow makes it easier for us to accept the disability as something special, something apart from other disabilities that somehow seem easier to get to grips with. This air of the exotic is so compelling as to even be the subject of movies – *Rainman*, for example, leading to a popular misconception that all people with autism have a wonderful talent, the 'You mean he can't count chopsticks thrown on the floor?' misunderstanding that so frustrates parents of children like Liam.

The second view of autism is at the other extreme. In this populist understanding autism is seen as a disability that completely isolates the individual from the regular world. Here the image is a bleak and frightening one of a child locked in a world of its own unable to relate to anyone. The idea of someone being unable to relate to his or her fellow human beings in any way is an awful one to contemplate. We are, after all, primarily social beings. We interact with and need other people around us to feel complete. The pleasures of social interaction are as natural to us as breathing. In this view of autism we are distressed at the thought of such lonely isolation. Pity is mingled with disbelief that anyone could face life being so afraid of other people. The desire to reach out and break down the barriers is strong. The corresponding frustration at not being able to do so leaves us with a hollow feeling of helplessness. These two extremes of what it means to be autistic were very prevalent in my early reading. Up to that point I had never knowingly met anyone with autism.

I was then invited to a newly transferred Unit for children with autism with a view to applying for a job there. During my visit a class of secondary age pupils with autism were on a pre-arranged visit to the head teacher's office, as part of a social skills lesson. There was a knock at the door and simultaneously, before the Head had time to say 'come in', a lanky young man in his teens marched into the room with a determined air and unceremoniously plonked himself on my knee. Sitting with his back to me he ignored all my attempts to be sociable.

The teacher and the rest of the class followed behind. One or two pupils sat down, others stood apparently helpless until the teacher and her assistant steered them towards chairs and encouraged them to sit. One boy, as if rooted to the floor, had to be led gently by the arm and nudged into place. A young lady said 'Hello' to the Head in a rather flustered, gushing voice. A painfully shy gangly lad, blushing to his core, also said 'Hello'. It was clear the effort of being sociable had been difficult. He looked painfully self-conscious and was unable to give eye contact to anyone as he spoke, but a gentle smile neverthe-less broke across his tense face. The teacher, with a quiet unassuming voice, called to the boy on my knee. She patted a seat next to her and told the boy to come and sit down. Without a backward glance he got up and slumped down in the chair. He did not look at the teacher or me. He said nothing.

Later I had a tour of the Unit. I remember the child who had a mouthful of leaves that he had grabbed at the end of playtime. They were now being extri-cated from his mouth. I sat next to a little boy who immediately got up and left the Lego model he had been so absorbed in. He stood a respectful distance away, watching us furtively from the safety of the far wall. A large boy leapt to his feet as soon as we entered his classroom, nearly knocking his chair over in his enthusiasm to give me a great bear hug. Another boy asked me my date of birth. Once given the information he appeared satisfied and went back to his work. The young lady who had spoken in the office was now head bent over a maths problem, muttering crossly to herself, whilst a rather sullen young man rocked aggressively back and forth on his chair. I remember the quiet confi-dence of the staff and the ease with which they dealt with the different situa-tions. All that I saw fitted well into the reading I had done and confirmed my preconceptions about autism.

Months later I became a member of the team. I was appointed as teacher for 'Class One'. It turned out to be the most interesting, rewarding and challeng-ing time of my life. This was exactly the job/vocation I had been searching for. I had become one of those lucky people for whom work married perfectly with my personality. I felt at home. Not that all that was apparent to me on my first day.

For example, on that first day not one child in my new class fell for my usual charms as a teacher. In fact many seemed to do everything they could to ignore me or, better still, make me go away. As a teacher who prided herself in her ability to strike up an instant rapport with even the shyest, most reluctant pupil, I have to admit I found this all rather disconcerting. It was unsettling to find I had no instant impact on a child despite my most tried and tested charm assault. Worse, it was positively distressing to discover that by doing nothing, just by being quietly, unassumingly myself, I could trigger a distressed tantrum that seemed to go on forever. It broke into all those preconceived ideas about myself that made me confident that I was, indeed, the sort of teacher that could make a valuable contribution to the education of these children.

It wasn't that I came to the job completely ignorant of autism. I have already explained that I had avidly read every one of the biographies that were available, every textbook that I could lay my hands on and every advice leaflet that the National Autistic Society had to give me. But none of the books prepared me for the simple fact that a child with autism is exactly that. A child.

I was not alone in this view. Toby's parents explain their impressions once Toby began school.

> ...I think of all the books that we read...you thought they [children with autism] were all sort of the same. But once he was in the school and you met more children and more parents you realise they are all totally individual. There is a style that runs through them all, but I suppose that is the same for everybody...

As you read about the seven children in my first class you will recognise the textbook features of autism (or 'the style' as Toby's parents so aptly describe it) but over and above that you will meet seven very distinct children with disparate personalities; children who are reacting to one another and to the social world of the classroom as individually as you would expect any children to react. The heights and depths of their reactions are what make this class of children different from any other class, and the job of teaching them so much more exciting.

Firmly committed to the notion that education is a journey for both learner and teacher I quickly adjusted my approach and soon discovered that I was, in fact, able to bring the same values, determination and sense of discovery into this small class of children with autism as I had to my other teaching experiences. It was the scale of the challenge that set it apart. Believing that it is better to have high expectations than low ones – the history of special education sadly suggests that low expectations have often held back both our understanding and our ability to help children develop to their full potential – I strove to make the classroom a lively successful learning forum where every achievement was valued and celebrated. Being part of a team was invaluable

here. The competent confidence of Sally and Erin, my two experienced teaching assistants, eased me gently into the hurly burly of classroom life and helped me maintain both a sense of proportion and a sense of humour. I was honest enough to admit that I did not know what to do, and Sally and Erin were kind enough to assure me that I was doing fine.

It was not long before I understood that all the children in my class could and did form relationships, however fragile or transient those relationships sometimes were. These relationships were all the more special because they blossomed despite a plethora of social and emotional difficulties conspiring against them. By their very nature they were subtle relationships, often not easily recognisable, certainly not as easygoing as regular relationships can be, but all the more precious for that. The privilege of trust and friendship was hard won, but once given it was discernible in every challenge, every upset, every frustration and every joy that the children experienced. Lotti's mum put it succinctly, when she talked about her developing relationship with her daughter.

> ...She paid more attention to the television than me – cartoons and that. I thought, if I put a cardboard box over my head she might look at me...but as soon as she gave that little bit back... I thought well yes you are – for all you might look as if you aren't taking notice – you are.

So I discovered that you don't have to be Rainman, you don't have to have an outstanding talent and you don't have to overcome your disability to be worthy of celebration. As you read about the delightful personalities of the children who are constantly striving to learn to live and be happy in our confusing social world I trust it will give you food for thought. Without their personalities, and without their autism, they would not be the people they are, and I for one would not have had my life enriched by them in the profound way that it has been. Getting to know these children has been a great privilege. It has shown me the importance of give and take in relationships no matter what point you start from.

This book strives to be a frank account of one small class of children with autism in all its rich variety, but above all it is a celebration of a very special community of teachers, parents and children who, at one time in their lives, were intimately woven together through many small but significant challenges and triumphs. I hope you enjoy getting to know the children and their families as much as I have.

Chapter 1

The Runner

Joss is a slight, elfin like boy, with huge brown eyes and long dark lashes. He was diagnosed with autism at three years and eight months and started full-time education when he was four years and ten months old. He occasionally uses single words to communicate but relies on leading adults towards his needs and wants. If upset or anxious he becomes very quiet and withdrawn. When he can hold back no longer he cries, but rejects comfort. Joss likes tickles and will hold hands and cuddle against you, on his terms. He likes lining up toys, running and counting.

Joss and I feel much the same by the end of our first day. Wrung out. The difference is that as we are singing the goodbye song I keep smiling, giving off vibes that I am in control of the situation, whereas Joss sits wide-eyed and silent, curled up like a tiny human ball. His bottom lip is quivering. He looks at his knees trying to shut out the chatter of children and adults that surround him. He angrily rebuffs comforting arms. He is desperately trying to be brave.

Alice, an old-timer and already standing out as the most cooperative member of the class, is the only child joining in the singing, albeit only spasmodically. Erin, one of my two indispensable teaching assistants, jollies her along. Sally, matter of fact and motherly, is preoccupied with making sure Lotti does not get over friendly with Nathan. Nathan is sitting with his back to the group studying the *Beano*. Toby is jumping excitedly up and down calling out 'see Clive, see Clive', the driver of the Orange Bus, whose arrival will signal the end of this first, long day. Alice, Toby, Lotti and Nathan are the four established members of the class. They have at least five years of collective classroom experience behind them. Liam and Sam, the other two 'new starters', are yet to join us. Someone, thankfully, has made the decision to stagger the start for the new children. By virtue of his age – or maybe in response to parental desperation – Joss is the first to join the established four, in what is known imaginatively as Class One.

Joss has no idea what to expect of his first day at school. Although I am an experienced mainstream teacher, I too am hardly prepared for the feelings I have at the end of my first day. In one day I have met with more professional, physical and emotional challenges than in a term at what I would have described as the challenging primary school I had just left. But I have a wealth of understanding and professional optimism to carry me through the day. Joss has autism. He has remained a silent, passive and wide-eyed boy throughout the day – an emotional closed book. I know that this day of challenges and strange new happenings will soon be over. Joss probably does not know if he will ever be back home again. He does not understand that after the singing he will get on the bus and be driven back to his family. All he knows is that his whole day has been a series of changing events and unfamiliar faces and now he has reached the limits of his limited coping strategies. He arrived in the morning, a fragile, silent little five-year-old. He made a beeline for the box of Duplo and busied himself lining up the cars and trucks end to end in a line that stretched across the classroom floor.

From that moment it becomes his favourite toy. He spends the rest of the day warding off adults and children alike from an imaginary but impenetrable barrier he creates around himself. Guarding his treasures like an over-vigilant security guard, his Dalek-like arm wards off any potential invaders.

Now, as he sits with his knees pressed up against his little chin, arms wrapped firmly around his legs, fingers locked tight, an air of sadness creeps over him like a fine mist. Uncomfortably poised between confident Alice and bouncy Toby, Joss's demeanour begins to change. He starts to fall apart. His large innocent eyes well up with tears. His soft delicate bottom lip, which has hardly moved all day, starts to tremble. His small slight shoulders begin to shake until, to our collective dismay, enormous tears spill over his long dark lashes and pour like a burst dam down his delicate bone china cheeks. Silent sobbing fills the room.

There is nothing anyone can do to console him. Keeping each of us at bay with a determined angry push, the silent tears keep falling. All the tension, anxiety and confusion of this, his first day at school, comes pouring out and threatens to overwhelm him. It is almost too much to bear, seeing him so unreachably unhappy.

Instinctively I want to wrap him up in my arms and reassure him that everything will be all right. But the steep learning curve that is my first day as a teacher of children with autism has already shown me that instinct and normal rules don't necessarily apply. Joss has made it abundantly clear that touch is not something that he finds comforting, and contact with kind people is a threat, not a consolation.

So, although my heart goes out to him, I have to suppress my instincts. Instead I continue in as calm and jolly a voice as I can muster to sing the goodbye song. I repeat, for all who may or may not understand, that as the pictures on our timetable show, after 'singing' it is time for 'bus' and 'home'. Knowing how emotionally wrung out I feel I can well appreciate that for a little boy with no language, little understanding and not a clue that soon he will be back with his mum, dad and big brother, the day has become simply too much to handle.

A few minutes earlier, I had confidently written that Joss had coped remarkably well with all the strange new routines and people he had met today. Up to the time of writing this had appeared true. Admittedly he had not let anyone too near him while he was playing with the train set. True, he had barely looked up from the floor, avoiding eye contact with everyone who tried to engage with him. But he had held hands to walk to the dinner hall. He had been out in the yard for a play. And he had sat at the table with us all, ready to listen to our goodbye song.

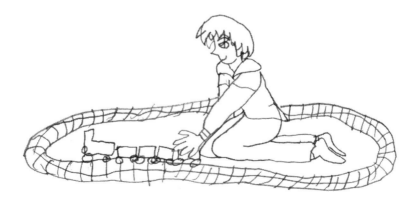

He had not said a word. But he does have severe communication problems, so that is understandable. In fact, it is three days before we really hear Joss speak, and when he does it is with such an apologetic, faraway little voice that if you aren't right next to him, listening out for it, you can easily mistake it for the whisper of the wind. And he hadn't cried. Until now.

It is no wonder, I thought, that this little scrap of a boy who cannot explain how he feels, cannot turn to anyone for comfort, does not understand what is about to happen, is crying. Even tough little boys with more language and bravado than is acceptable on a first day at school can suffer the wobbles for mum when home time finally looms.

Joss is going home to his mum. I can well imagine what a long day it has been for her too, wondering anxiously whether her little boy is in caring, understanding hands. The tears continue to fall, droplets of sadness that had it not been for the arrival of Clive and the longed for 'Orange Bus' I would be adding to with my own tears, not only in sympathy but also out of the unfamiliar helplessness I feel wanting to reach out and comfort this little boy, but knowing that it will only cause him greater distress. It is an uncomfortable feeling, this helplessness. I have always been able to establish a rapport with children and quickly make them feel at ease with me. It is disconcerting to feel so deskilled in such a fundamental way. This feeling of helplessness is, of course, all too familiar to anyone trying to make contact with a child with autism, a child who is unable to accept the natural comfort that a hug and a kind word can give. It is a helplessness that I will experience again and again while working with these children, but never with the intensity of this first day. Gradually, I learn to accept that it is inevitable that in any relationship with children so complex and individual I will experience both emotional highs and lows as together we try to make sense of this enigma called autism. So it is that Joss and I end our first day. Emotionally exhausted and with barely time to turn around before it starts again.

Of course, neither Joss nor I stay in this fragile state for long, I am pleased to say. However, throughout that year, as we both develop strategies for coping with the complexities of autism in a busy classroom and gain confidence in our new status, he as pupil, me as teacher, he will occasionally have moments when that hidden well of emotion will overwhelm him and he will weep silently and inconsolably. And at those times I will watch, as helpless as on that first day to stem the flow of his private unhappiness.

In time, after 'the honeymoon period' is over, Joss's other personality emerges. As he finds his feet we discover the flip side of the silent self-contained boy. Joss loves to run. Fast. And climb. And jump. And giggle and quiver with excitement. Excitement from escaping. I begin to suspect that those early days, those fragile early days, have merely been a front, behind which Joss has been methodically sussing out the lay of the land and making plans.

It begins innocently enough. The occasional bolt out of the classroom door and down the corridor, where a locked door prevents further distance. This is easy to deal with. I tear after him, take his hand and lead him, his little body quivering with giggles, big eyes gleefully glinting, calmly back to the classroom. Joss seems to think this is what being in school is all about. We confer. We decide, giving him the benefit of the doubt, that it is his way of avoiding tricky situations (touching sticky dough during cooking, perhaps, or not wanting to finish a jigsaw). It is his way of communicating with us. We are used to trying to interpret non-communicative behaviour and this seems a reasonable assumption. It does not, in fact, hold water. The bolts out of the classroom become more frequent. They appear to be linked not so much with anxiety as with opportunity and a good mood. The novelty of fetching him back begins to wear thin. We confer again.

He does seem to rather like the chase, we agree. We try a different tack. We decide to remove the drama – the chase, the chastising, the whole noise and fuss. We think that if we are more nonchalant about bringing him back, if we don't give him the satisfaction of knowing he is being chased, then he won't get so giggly and the fun will go out of it for him. It's a well-tried strategy. It is in lots of the books about behaviour management. It has worked for other children. It seems both plausible and practical. In reality, it merely gives him more time to do the running, to end up in another classroom, or the office or even, joy of joys, the Soft Play Room. And it is nearly impossible to be nonchalant when returning to the classroom. Joss is so happy on these occasions that he gives his best (conspiratorial) eye contact, makes the most open attempts at sharing a moment and is, frankly, so disarmingly sweet with his gleefully mischievous grin and his bouncy chuckling body that inevitably he breaks down our carefully composed demeanour. Once he sees even the faintest smile escape from our lips he knows that victory is his. As he returns to the classroom he is one very happy child.

Outwitted, we realise that we will have to revise our strategy. 'Why not make it more difficult to get out?' seems an obvious question inviting a simple solution. A bit of classroom reorganisation and we manage to create a challenging route involving a bit of climbing, a bit of jumping, a wriggle here, a squeeze there. The theory is that we will have time to distract him in the classroom before he gets out of the door. In practice, the minute our backs are turned to deal with some drama or other (and it will become evident that dramas practically fill our working days) Joss is off. He just loves the extra challenge. His squeals of delight alert us to his skilful exit. If he could articulate his opinion about the new classroom layout, contrary to all the textbooks that state categorically that 'children with autism do not like change', I am sure he would thank us profusely for making his escape so much more satisfyingly challenging.

We are, of course, very much aware of the downside of this aspect of Joss's character. He has absolutely no sense of danger. Within the safe environs of school we can contain his impulses. We do, of course, try to do more than that. While I have painted a picture of Joss's emerging confidence and successful outwitting of our attempts to keep him within the four walls of the classroom, we learn from Joss and try to develop in him a sense of self-control.

The PE hall is a considerable distance from the classroom. It involves going through locked doors that separate us from the main part of the school. While walking to the hall it is possible to run away in three different directions. All lead ultimately to unlocked doors, and escape to school fields or the school car park. So we are very vigilant. We realise Joss needs to have his hand held to make it safely into the hall. He becomes extremely giggly on these occasions, and it soon becomes clear he is constantly thinking about the possibility of escaping. To break this obsession, and encourage some self-control (something his mother is understandably very anxious for him to develop), we begin to encourage Joss to walk alone, forcing him to take control of himself instead of always relying on us. He responds well to this. When he is able to curb his impulse to run through the corridors and enter the PE hall calmly we reward him with a chase around the PE hall and lots of smiles and jumping about, which he loves. Of course, someone is always within a whisker of him when he is going it alone, nonchalantly nearby, poised like a spring to grab him should his impulses get the better of him. Gradually, he is able to make the trek from classroom to hall without the need for such close supervision. We are pleased with this progress, but know it is fragile. For the more sociable and happy Joss is, the more alert we are to the possibility of an escape. We are learning to read the signs. Pleased as we are with his progress, Joss is a long way from being in control of his impulse to run and it simmers below the surface most days, especially when he is happy.

But at least we know he is safe and within our grasp. We are now alert to his moods and know the parts of the school where we have to be extra vigilant. The locked door at the end of the corridor ensures that during class time at the very least it is only an inconvenience to fetch him and at most an irritation to be continually outwitted by a sweet, sensitive five-year-old. So we manage. It becomes part of the possibility of our day. And for a while, Joss is satisfied with this level of adventure. But Joss has ambitions. The corridor is one thing. The Great Outdoors is something else.

If I have been doing Joss an injustice to suggest that in those early, uncertain days at the beginning of term Joss might have been planning his Corridor Great Escape Plan, I have no such reservations about Joss's next venture. This had to be the culmination of a well thought-out strategy. How else could he have co-ordinated time, place and action so cleverly?

I have already mentioned that the corridor ended with a locked door. We go through this door to the PE hall, as explained. The corridor also leads to the dinner hall, which is in fact a vast open space with three possible escape routes from it. Fortunately the serving area and our tables are well away from the escape routes and we are amply provided with dinner staff to help us during this potentially fraught time. We are all alerted to the possibility these escape routes offer and Joss is kept busy and focused on the business of getting and eating his dinner.

The serving area is in front of the kitchen, the doors of which are open to allow the free passage of trays of potatoes, funny face fish cakes, dinosaur burgers and the obligatory boiled cabbage that graces the dining halls of schools the length and breadth of the country. At the back of the kitchen, barely visible from the hall, is a door that opens up onto the car park. This door is usually shut, but on hot days (which, as you will appreciate, are few and far between) Lorna, our relentlessly cheerful cook, will leave it open. Not that any of us are aware of this fact – yet. If we had been aware, we would have noted that it is only possible to see a sliver of daylight, barely a hint of an enticing outdoor world. It is certainly not a great open invitation. But we are not aware. It just isn't the sort of thing you take notice of in the normal run of school mealtimes when your concentration is focused on helping seven children through the ritual of choosing dinner, pudding and a drink from an array of choices they can't even see because their little noses barely reach up to the tops of the serving counter.

Because of their age and their differing communication difficulties every child in the class needs help at dinnertime and we are well served with extra

dinner staff. Everyone has very particular needs regarding food choice. It is rare for children with autism to like variety in their diet and our class are no exception. The challenge is to remember what each one likes or, more importantly, dislikes, since any infringement onto the tray of unwanted food items or unacceptable combinations of foods can lead to one of several responses (in increasing order of potential disaster):

- loud squeals of disapproval expressed in no uncertain terms: 'Take them off, they make me sick' (Alice's preferred response)

- adamant refusal to move tray and self along the food counter until offending item(s) are removed (Toby)

- throwing the food back at the server in disgust (Lotti)

- standing passively as tray is filled by adult, all the while trying to contain disappointment, until point is reached when unstoppable tears flow (Joss)

- dropping self onto floor and having major tantrum until clean tray with correct food is satisfactorily presented (Nathan).

As can be appreciated, we adults work hard to avoid the need for any of these responses by remembering, guiding, guessing and, ultimately, hoping that we have learned and remembered the particular gastronomic quirks of the child we are helping that day. Dinnertimes, then, are potentially fraught occasions and we put all our concentration into ensuring that each child arrives at a table happy and ready to eat their chosen fare. It is fair to say that no attention is given by us to look out for gaps in doors barely visible through other doors and food counters.

Joss is passive about what goes on his tray in the early days and it is difficult to assess his likes and dislikes without him dissolving into those silent sobs that so defeat any attempts to comfort him. At least with a tantrum it is clear when the mistakes have been rectified. With Joss, the tears often continue to fall long after the problem has been sorted, leaving a trail of false clues that make it difficult for us to remedy his predicament. It takes a long time to get it right. The hardest thing to understand is that funny face fish cakes with mashed potatoes are *exactly* what Joss loves, but only if the fish cake is on one side of the tray and the mashed potato on the opposite side so that neither touch one another.

The tears make us feel very protective towards Joss. It is unimaginably sad to know he is struggling to communicate, without words, something that is of such importance to him. We all agree that these silent tears make us feel more helpless than a tantrum does, as they seem to come from the very depths of his soul and only begin to fall after Joss has lost the battle for self-control that rages within him, rendering him finally emotionally exposed. I think this feeds our belief that Joss is a vulnerable little waif who needs our protection. It is very gratifying seeing him make increasing steps towards independence. As term progresses Joss is able to move confidently along the food counter to collect a funny face fish cake, mashed potato (placed carefully next to, not touching, the funny face), toffee yoghurt and a drink of milk. Then, with only minimum help, he will wend his way between tables and children and settle down to begin his dinner.

On this particular day Joss is smiling and giggling, giving lots of eye contact and generally being very happy with life. Alarm bells should have rung, if only faintly. But it is one of those good days when no one is upset; everyone is happy. Everything is going swimmingly. The children are all getting on with the business of choosing their food and settling down to eat. Looking at Joss's happy demeanour gives me considerable pleasure. He is defi-nitely settled in his new class and it is satisfying to see him jiggle and giggle his way along the counters to choose the foods he enjoys. Lorna reminds the new potato server to put his scoop next to but not touching ('he don't like that') his fish cake. Joss carefully picks out his favourite toffee flavoured yoghurt – another step towards independence, I note. I smile encouragingly back as Joss turns with his milk carefully balanced on his tray to walk towards his table, following close behind me.

Crash! Milk splashes up my legs and the soft plop of mashed potato splat-ters on the floor. Exasperated that Joss's happiness is about to be snatched from him by an accident that will almost certainly reduce him to silent sobs, I turn to reassure and comfort the little boy. He isn't there. As I move forward my foot slips on the mashed potato and milky goo spreading over the floor and I slide unceremoniously onto my bottom. I yell 'Joss' as, ducking and diving between the tight array of tables, chairs, children and staff, I catch a glimpse of Joss's bottom disappearing under the serving counter and into the kitchen. He is making his bid for freedom. My attempts to swiftly follow are thwarted by the slippery mix of congealing mashed potato and milk and I barely manage to stay upright, let alone go in hot pursuit of the wily fugitive. His escape route effectively clear and with the element of surprise and chaos giving him a distinct advantage, Joss makes it to the back of the kitchen, to the door he has seen that has been left ever so slightly open. With a whoop of delight Joss dashes through the door and triumphantly finds himself in the Great Outdoors of the school car park.

Thankfully, his strategy fails him at this point. He pauses. Whether this is because he has achieved his goal, or whether he needs time to assess the unfamiliar layout of the car park before fleeing victoriously into the Great Beyond, we will never know. Before he has time to move, Lorna, who has just returned to the kitchen to get more fish cakes, registers first the whoop of delight and then the slight figure of Joss disappearing through the now wide open door. She hurls herself outside and catches up with him.

Joss is not upset at being caught. There are no tears. No attempt to pull away. He gives no signs of disappointment or frustration at the outcome of his little escapade. On the contrary he takes his capture with equanimity and is led back as giggly and happy as he was a few minutes earlier with dinner in hand and a hall full of staff to care for him. The staff are considerably shaken.

Joss spends the rest of the day chuckling gleefully to himself. His autism apparently does not prevent him from enjoying the recall of the adrenalin rush he must have experienced in those brief but glorious moments of escape. I am sure he is revelling in the exhilaration of a plan well executed. He bears us no grudges, remaining in good humour throughout the day. He never tries to escape that way again – we never give him the opportunity. Security is tightened and an ever more thorough recce of potential escape routes is now our first priority wherever we go. It becomes increasingly difficult to keep one step ahead of him, and it becomes a nagging worry that one day he may come to harm.

Joss continues to keep us on our toes. We learn to be suspicious of his hyper giggly states, remembering how they can lull us into a false sense of security. But Joss continues to be Joss, wide-eyed and innocent looking. His sad still self still engenders feelings of protectiveness in us and he continues to beguile us with his quiet gentle ways.

To be fair, Joss's next adventure comes about more through our fault than through his planning, as we are well aware of his desire to climb the fence. This state of affairs comes about as a result of a sad lack of interesting and stimulating playground equipment, a source of much frustration to staff and pupils alike. A year ago a wooden climbing frame that was well used and liked by many pupils was vandalised and burned down. With neither money nor a clear strategy of how to avoid a similar fate happening to new equipment, plus a mountain of bureaucratic indifference and an array of Health and Safety issues darkening the way forward, the playground is, frankly, boring.

Of course, there are a few children for whom an unimaginative piece of tarmac, with grass along one edge and an array of trees and bushes separating it from the outside world on two sides, is exciting enough. These are the children who are happy enough to stalk the perimeter fences admiring the patterns of light on metal or who like to stand engrossed with a piece of string or a blade of grass deep in their unfathomable autistic world view.

Children with autism are not good at making up games with friends, devising imaginary worlds that transform a dull playground into an adventure wonderland that accommodates endless varieties of imaginative games. We buy an array of freestanding play equipment. Gradually, these toys dwindle in number and variety as children find new and generally worrying uses for them. Bolts become mysteriously unscrewed from bikes, rendering them lethal; balls are thrown over the fence at the row of parked cars; children become hysterical over the need to turn take; one of the larger lads finds it very enjoyable to lift up the wheeled tyre and hurl it at the fence, for the pleasure of hearing it rattle. The large toys are gradually withdrawn to safeguard the lives of others and soft balls that can do no damage to cars are substituted. We all wait for the money to turn the yard into a safe and fun-filled playground again.

Joss arrives when playground distractions have reached an all-time low. He is neither a pacer nor a ball thrower. He likes to climb. So it is that Joss learns to climb the chain link fence between the yard and the inner courtyard of the school. It is the only thing left in the playground with any challenge factor to it. Of course, as soon as we see this, we discourage him, offering him enticing games with the light balls, or interesting chases around the grass. However, a child with autism who has an ambition will not allow anyone or anything to deter him from his chosen activity. Joss humours us but time and again he makes it to the fence. Time and again staff on playground duty lead him away and it becomes a major preoccupation to deter Joss from climbing the chain link fence. It becomes a huge frustration that we have nothing that will prove more attractive than the fence to lure him from it. We curse the vandals and wait hopefully for money to build a new, flame-proof climbing frame. All the while Joss continues his obsession with the chain link fence, gaining greater and greater height at each snatched opportunity. We comfort ourselves with the fact that it will be impossible to actually get over the top, as the fence is angled to deter the vandals. (How come that doesn't set alarm bells ringing?)

We continue to thwart his heart's desire. He tries hard to devise opportunities to get to and over the fence before we catch up with him. He tries to be the first out, hoping that the time lag will give him the necessary head start, but it is never quite enough. He tries distracting staff. One innocent little remark 'Look, aeroplane' both charms and thrills us, as it is the first time we have heard Joss put two words together *and* engage with an adult for a shared experience. We are very moved. While we are being moved, gazing up at the aeroplane and doing appropriate teacher activity, like extending the language and acknowledging the personal exchange 'Yes Joss, I can see the aeroplane too. Isn't it high?', Joss has gained an advantage and manages to get ever closer to his goal of the top of the fence. But again we are too quick for him and with good grace he climbs back down and giggles off to hang around near the bushes. He likes to disappear behind the bushes, along with a few others. It is like a little den. Given the lack of other excitement in the yard we are happy to tolerate this, as it is possible to see what is going on from the sidelines. But to be fair, I think we all know, Joss and the staff, that it is only a matter of time before opportunity and talent will get the better of us.

Eventually, the day arrives, as we knew it would. A crisis happens that takes the full attention of the three staff on duty and Joss shamelessly takes advantage of us in the seconds before back-up staff arrive. It is a great shock to see Joss running past us on the other side of the fence and it takes several bemused moments to react, run through the corridor to the entrance hall, open the French windows that lead onto the inner courtyard and catch him. As we race after him, unsuitably dressed for a mini marathon in smart shoes and tight skirt – no match for Joss in his trainers and shorts – Joss's enjoyment increases. Gleefully glancing back at us, puffing, panting and shouting (wasting precious breath and time in the process), Joss continues to have the advantage for several metres. Like a rabbit looking for its burrow, he gives little leaps of sheer exuberance. This is what school should be about!

But he is still only five, and we are adults. He may have the relative speed advantage, but we have longer legs and a bigger incentive to bring this chase to an end. It will be one thing explaining to his mum that he has climbed the fence and escaped, but the humiliation of having to admit that little Joss can outrun us spurs us into greater effort and we finally catch up with him.

We are, naturally, too short of breath by now to say anything to him about the seriousness of his crime, but to be frank, what would have been the point?

Joss is Joss. Running is his joy. He has a joyful few minutes (is that all? It feels like a lifetime) and now he is safe. And for a boy with so few real pleasures in life, is it fair to take away his obvious delight in the freedom and exhilaration he has had as he raced across the playing field in wonderful abandonment? And boy, is he pleased with himself! This is his greatest achievement yet, and he loves it. He comes back to school happier than he has ever been, skipping, jumping, giggling and laughing. Of course we do struggle to do our adult duty to be cross with him. We try to impress on him the seriousness of his crime. We make picture communications about not running, not climbing, keeping safe. We are realistic, however. We know we are making only the most superficial of impressions. We understand that this is Joss. He is oblivious to our concerns.

The rest of his day, as before, is spent reliving the moments, the smile of satisfaction beaming across his face emanating blissful fulfilment of his dream. Singing our goodbye song that night, Joss certainly doesn't cry and he positively skips onto the Orange Bus. As he waves goodbye a shiver of glee runs through him. Without any verbal communication he leaves us in no doubt at all that today has been one of his best days at school so far! As we wave goodbye we turn to join the rest of the staff for a meeting. Top of the Agenda is 'Playground Safety'. And this is only his first year!

Despite all the inconvenience and worry Joss puts us through with his escapades one thing is certain. To see Joss giggling and happy after one of his adventures (whether minor or major) is to see his spirit in action. Beyond the silent, withdrawn, emotionally overwhelmed Joss is a mischievous little boy who finds expression in a way that many little boys without his severe difficulties would relate to and cheer. A child without autism may be better deterred by an adult's remonstrations. They may lower their ambitions in the light of what is socially acceptable (every five-year-old learns that you stay in class until the bell goes, however boring Miss Smith's explanation of number bonds is, if you want to be let out for playtime). They know how to adjust their desires to conform to the norms around. Transgressions are usually minor ('Don't do that, George') and behaviour modified in the light of potential recriminations. Very few five-year-olds are prepared to miss playtime, for example.

Joss works outside the social mores of five-year-old classroom behaviour, so his steps towards stamping his individuality on his environment are more dramatic and the consequences of his actions more far reaching. But without this expression of self, he would be left with only the inward sadness and its outward manifestation of silent tears. If Joss were to lose that giggle; that desire to be bold and fearless; that love of running and the thrill of the chase; the satisfaction of a well-executed plan; in short, if Joss were to lose his spirit what would be left? Probably no more than an unhappy, withdrawn, spiritless child.

So, when Joss comes to school, eyes cast down, bottom lip trembling, arms rigidly pushing us away, we do what we can to bring out the spirit in him. And as we chase after him down the corridor for the hundredth time, we almost cheer him on, hopeful that we are seeing Joss as his true self.

Joss's mum tells of the worries concerning Joss and his love of running

"Running was a huge concern, always has been, always will be because the school wasn't as safe as it is now, only because he's tested it to the limits. He's tested school to the limits and every time he's done something they've had to realise just how smart he is for working things out.

It's all for the chase now. It's really, really, really annoying when he does it. I just think 'you are being just naughty'. But when he was little, with you, I used to think 'Well, he can't help it. He doesn't know what he is doing is wrong. He doesn't understand that he has got all this energy and he shouldn't be just dashing off everywhere. He has no idea about danger or anything.'

He's always liked the chase. He's always done it for the chase. And do you know what I think it is? You know *Bedknobs and Broomsticks?* Well...the witch turns somebody into something and she ends up turning one of the children into a rabbit and the cat chases the rabbit up the stairs, round the house, then all of a sudden the boy (who's been changed into a rabbit) changes back into a boy and starts chasing the cat. So there's this great big chase thing going on and he's loved that film. He's always loved that film. He does it now, in here. You can see him, he's acting out that scene and he's dashing down the stairs and he just thinks it's hilarious and it's all to do with the video. He loves being chased and thinks it's absolutely the best thing when someone is chasing him. I know he knows but all those years ago he didn't. He just had to do it.

...If I thought he could cross the road, if I thought he had any road sense whatsoever, it wouldn't worry me half as much as it does, but the fact that he doesn't have any, I just think oh god...

I think he was *driven to do it*. I think when he was little it was all that gluten and whatever was going on with the blood and casein. You know, all this stuff

)lood – going into the brain through his blood stream that
ing in. But that's a lot more under control now…mind he's
t [the running] for years. It's maybe taken years to get it out of

Starting school

"…I didn't want him to go anywhere else. I didn't want him to go away. I knew he couldn't go in the ordinary school. He just couldn't. I didn't know about the special needs schools. I wanted somewhere that was autism specific.

…I wanted somewhere that was safe. Safety was the first issue. I knew it had to be safe and I thought the Unit was safe. It's only when he did things that I realised he wasn't safe. He's done things recently where they've had to make adjustments because of the way he's got out. So, safety. And I wanted people who knew about autism and could do something else than toilet train him. I just thought that was such a massive step when he was toilet trained that I thought, maybe he's never had any other professional input before, apart from this speech therapy class with about eight other kids. It was just chaos. They just ran round screaming. It was bedlam. It was a waste of time, totally.

…Being safe really was the overriding issue for everything. I really wouldn't have cared what the school was like as long as it was safe, as long as I knew he was going there and he was going to be all right…some of the time it wasn't as safe as it could be.

…He's got to do it or attempt to before you realise he has that capability. I mean I never went round school and said 'he will be able to get round there and over there and through this and don't do that'…so I know that he would do things that you wouldn't expect him to do like to be able to climb over that fence. I didn't know he would do that and he would do it when you least expect him to.

…We used to absolutely love it when he was ill. He'd be laid on the sofa because he wasn't very well – I mean there weren't many of those days – but we used to think god this is *absolutely gorgeous*, because he was safe. He didn't want to do anything and it was just peace, perfect peace. None of this charging around like a whirlwind…it used to do my head in. It used to absolutely crack me up. You just couldn't take your eyes off him for a second. I used to have to follow him everywhere. I used to have to follow him. Everything he did he had to be constantly supervised. I couldn't go in the shower unless [my husband] was here to watch him. Anything really, you couldn't come in here to cook the tea without [my husband] being in there or in here while I was out there to look after him. [By the time he went to school] I basically wanted rid of him, to give him to someone else for five days a week. He was a worry. I think I was just relieved to have him in a school, to have him in a school that I wanted to have him in, that was right.

I like to know that the people who work with him care about him [very distressed]…and the way people would talk to me about him I used to think oh he's really getting on your nerves…

…I used to compare him to what everybody else was like and what they were doing and if one of them took a tantrum, I used to think 'yes, he's just like little Joss'…he's not the only one. He's not the worst, after all. Because that's what it sometimes felt like, that he was the absolute worse. Well, he is still sometimes, the worse out of any person who's ever been autistic.

I never had any concerns [about the class]. I just always thought he was safe and that you three did care about him, maybe because he was little as well. He was only little. He was only five, so he did have his canny days occasionally…

I always thought that you would have it so much in control – that he would never get in that situation where he would get out and go and be away. I always thought if he did get out, if he did get away, you'd easily be able to get hold of him and so on… But I mean, you really had to keep tight hold of him when you went out. So, when he was little I did used to think 'Oh I wish they just wouldn't go out' and then I thought you were trying to help him taking him out. But it was a worry…I always thought 'Yes, he might get on the road. There's a chance he might get run over.' But as for him getting lost or someone being able to, like, take him that never entered my head because I thought if he does go there is going to be someone after him like straight away… Now, I don't want him to be fit. I don't want him to be fit and fast and athletic… I would always have said that that school should do much more exercise in the day but it just dawned on me recently that the more exercise he gets, the fitter he's going to get… I don't want him to be fit. I want him to lie on the sofa and think I can't be bothered to do that… Say he didn't have that running away thing, then yes…I would want him to be fit…but it's just dawned on me that the more unfit he is the more he'll be inclined to think oh I can't be bothered to run so…but on the other hand I don't want him unfit and unhealthy. I'd like him to be fit and healthy. It is a dilemma, but I'll opt for the 'oh I'm too fat to run'.

…When he's happy it would set alarm bells because it means he's planning something, but I didn't realise what he could get up to, what he could do, so I used to think 'Oh, he'll be getting up to something' but I didn't really think he's going to end up running away or getting lost. But I preferred him to be happy and naughty – I don't know if I want him to be unhappy and good or unhappy and naughty. I don't know. It's a dilemma. Oh, he's one on his own, little Joss, he is!"

Chapter 2

Our Little Princess

Alice has short dark hair and a round face with brown eyes and freckles. She would love to look like Snow White or Sleeping Beauty but in reality she is a plump and rather tomboyish little girl. Alice has good communication skills although she has difficulty using and understanding language flexibly. Outwardly friendly, she struggles to understand and conform to social rules and can be quite dramatic and vocal when things confuse or upset her. She loves drawing princesses. She can be mischievous but also charming.

Alice stands out on that first day – the day that Joss's sadness and my inability to lessen it threaten to overwhelm us both. She seems to be a very capable and cooperative little girl. I am both surprised and relieved to have her in the class. Surprised because I have little idea that a child with autism can relate to anyone as well as she appears to. Relieved because, as every teacher will admit (if only secretly), every classroom needs one such child – a child that wants to cooperate; will at the very least attempt to do the work you set; and best of all with a desire to earn praise and favour from the teacher. In a class as lively as mine, to have one child who, in my rather naive judgement, can apparently be relied on to conform feels like a godsend.

Of course, when I say relied on, I should qualify that. There are, on that first day, five children. Three have severe communication problems, one can make himself understood, but in a unique and often cryptic fashion; four have behavioural problems which range from wanting to be left alone no matter what, to being hyperactive and needing constant watching. Then there is Alice.

It is true that Alice can complain loudly and dramatically about not wanting to do this task or that. It is also true that Alice can flounce as well as the most moody and seasoned teenager (although she is only six). But of all the children, she is the only one who says 'Hello Fran' and who follows my instructions with ease. I am too caught up with the general chaos to notice the gentle, kindly support Alice is being discreetly given by the more knowing teaching assistants who have worked with Alice for a year before my arrival and know she is less capable than I give her credit for on that first day. Like many people unfamiliar with autism, I make the mistake of assuming that because her language skills are good, her understanding of meaning and intention are equally advanced. I learn, in time, that Alice's apparent confidence masks a problem with social and emotional understanding that can make life very difficult for her. I am still very aware, and very grateful, that Alice can at least be *persuaded* to conform.

As I have already mentioned, Erin and Sally have worked with Alice for a year and know just how to do that talking round. I have not appreciated just how hard they are working behind the scenes to keep Alice sweet and to persuade her to be on her best behaviour (i.e. 'behave like a princess') on this first fraught day. In time, I too understand that there are certain ways of talking to Alice that encourage cooperation and compliance and it is not long before I too employ these techniques shamelessly when the need arises. But more of that later. For the moment I am simply grateful that there is one child who is being cooperative and responsive to my ever-dwindling array of skills, brought from my years in a mainstream classroom to this small lively bunch of kids.

So, while Nathan twirls around like a slippery snake when asked to sit at the table, Joss attacks with his Dalek-like arm if we attempt to get near him, Toby leaps on and off his chair like an over-excited jack-in-the-box and Lotti gnashes her teeth and threatens to pinch anyone who upsets her with unwelcome noises (i.e. Toby or Nathan – one with a too happy tone of voice, the other with too squealing a tone), Alice is gratifyingly cooperative. Of all the children, she alone can be relied on to sit still and wait patiently in her seat at the 'Round Table' – the focus of group participation – whilst we chase after the other children like demented sheepdogs trying to round up a flock of particularly bolshie sheep!

The reason we gather around the Round Table is for our daily story-time. Initially this is an event I dread, as it appears that nobody is in the least bit interested in hearing a story. Indeed, hadn't I read that this was so? And wasn't the complete absence of books in the classroom further proof that these children were only interested in books to tear them, throw them or repetitively stare at one page over and over? Once again, Alice appears to be the exception. She enjoys being read to and will listen to stories from start to finish. But it seems everyone else is focused on anything but the bright, colourful book I hold before me.

My usual opening gambit, said in a bright and breezy voice, 'Oh, look at this picture, what do you think this story is about?' – a line that had served me well enough in my previous teaching experience – here elicits a range of responses, from blank indifference to determined efforts to grab the book and use it as a missile. It confirms everything I have read about children with autism. Why should they be interested in a story about unreal happenings when they have no communication skills, no understanding of social exchanges and no imaginations? Perhaps we should just stick to singing, where at least the rhythm and actions seem to have a calming effect. But I really enjoy story-time. I want these children to learn to love it too. After all, what can be a richer language experience, a greater social event, and a more exciting glimpse into the world of the imagination than the shared experience of a good book?

So I struggle on. Alice responds. Not to the story, you understand, but to my lack of any semblance of order. Alice encouragingly, and with a slightly patronising edge to her voice, comments, 'Fran, Joss is trying to go under the table' and 'Fran, I don't think Lotti is very happy', as Lotti launches herself, teeth gnashing, at a hapless Erin, already struggling to prevent Toby from taking Nathan's comic in an act fuelled by mischief and indifference to the enriching qualities of literature.

I refuse to be defeated. Once again, after a steep learning curve, I discover that things that hold true with other children also hold true here, just on a different scale. These children can and do enjoy being read to, but everything has to be so much bolder, brighter and larger than life. All that is necessary is to choose a book and then learn to read it the right way. Up the drama, exaggerate the actions, ensure the story is rich in repetition, make the voices distinct and different, build up the rhythm, keep a good pace going and most important of all choose good stories.

They say teachers are thwarted actors. I have never had any desire to be on stage, but I know (Sally and Erin have told me) that I put everything I have into storytelling, and I have become as dramatic and theatrical as necessary to engage the children in an enjoyable book experience.

Fortunately there is a wealth of excellent books to choose from (see Appendix 1). It is not long before every child has his or her own particular favourites. For Nathan it is 'We're going on a Bear Hunt' – great rhythm, wonderful actions and an ending that can have Nathan wide-eyed on the edge of his seat every time he hears it, barely able to contain his excitement when we get to the part where the bear roars. Joss loves all books with counting in, such as 'Ten Little Bears' and 'The Hungry Cat'. Rote counting is often an area of learning where children with autism are particularly successful, so tapping into this is a great way of introducing books and the pleasure of reading and listening to stories.

Toby loves anything that means he can shout out, such as 'Wake Up Farmer George!' and 'Lullabyhullabaloo'. He also loves action books and these are great for channelling his considerable energies. Lotti likes stories with a singsong text and a strong beat, such as 'There was an Old Woman', and any book with bold bright pictures, that can excite and delight her with an intensity that is enviable. So we build up a library of books, and as the children learn to love the stories so they learn to respect books. Understanding more about how books work, they begin to choose books spontaneously from the book box that now has pride of place in the classroom. I am always delighted to see any of these children, who struggle with so much, get a book and find a quiet place to enjoy it at their level – whether that means staring over and over at a picture, or turning the pages rapidly, or reciting, with accurate intonation but unintelligible diction, the whole story. It is exciting to have opened up another interest for a child who is often locked in repetitive behaviour. The fact that none of these children would score on a comprehension test about the books they read in no way diminishes the satisfaction of having introduced them to books and opened up another world, however it is they choose to interpret and get pleasure from that world.

Once we have built up a library of fun stories that grab the attention of our discerning listeners we introduce the notion that each child can take turns to choose a book. This is sometimes challenging, as one child's choice does not necessarily please all, but it is an invaluable social experience, and as time goes by, and everyone understands that their turn will come, a level of tolerance and interest in others' choices enriches the value of story-time further. Once a story is in full swing, it is usually possible to engage all at some level, with a combination of exaggerated actions, funny voices, bright pictures and repeated phrases. It is only when Alice chooses her favourite book that we have a problem.

Alice, like so many little girls of her age, dreams of being a princess and her choice of story is always about one of the well-known princesses of the fairytales. Alice likes traditional, rather pedestrian, fairy tales as retold by Ladybird. Alice does not care one jot if no one else is interested in tales of beautiful young damsels in distress. Of course, the rest of the class are totally disinterested. They see no reason why they should spare Alice's (or anyone else's) feelings about this. They show their disinterest, as always, by their behaviour, none of which is polite or reasonable. Although I do not squeal, jump up and down on my chair, try to hide under the table or attempt to attack my nearest neighbour, I must admit to having some sympathy for their responses. I have come to love the buzz of reading bright, lively, funny stories that encourage a wealth of unimagined responses from these children with their unique, bizarre, funny take on life.

Alice doesn't care what we think. She does not concern herself with the fact that Sally and Erin are faced with an uphill struggle to keep the attention of her disinterested and restless classmates. She cannot conceive that they, like her, are not utterly enchanted with these tales of beautiful princesses beating all the odds to win the hand of a handsome prince.

It doesn't bother her that the stories she chooses have no bright pictures, lack strong rhythmic text and involve no counting (although I do try to emphasise that there are seven dwarves – but as we are not allowed to count them Joss is unimpressed even with this fact). For Alice knows her stories off by heart and they have to be read from cover to cover without repetition, deviation or hesitation. I do my best to try to make the stories go with a bit more panazz, but the material I am working with and Alice's strict parameters make it very difficult. For her, these tales have to be strictly of the 'Once upon a time…and they all lived happily ever after' variety and I think she genuinely relates to the rather old-fashioned language of the Ladybird tales.

We try a different tack. We seek out all the princess-related books we can find that might satisfy the criteria for a successful read. We introduce new stories about more gutsy princesses, the sort that scream and throw tantrums, such as the wonderful little princess of Tony Ross's creation. All the children love the story, because the little princess screams at the top of her voice 'I want my potty' and all the courtiers shout to one another 'She wants her potty!'

After several sessions of me, Sally and Erin pretending to be an array of characters and startling and amusing the children with our range of funny voices, this story becomes a wonderful starting point for social interaction and confidence building. The book comes with a little rag-doll princess complete with bright green potty, that we pass around the table, as a variety of characters, from the admiral to the cook, call out 'She wants her potty!' To hear the bold, but barely audible shout of 'She wants her potty' come from the usually silent Joss is one of my more treasured moments as a teacher, along with the sight of Lotti, who up to that point has never shown the slightest interest in dolls, or pretend play, tipping the princess off her potty and exclaiming 'Oh dear' in a deep, playful voice. Even Nathan and Toby call a truce to solemnly pass the princess to one another, giving her a parting kiss along the way. This was truly story-time at its best, and 'I want my potty' becomes one of the class's all-time favourites.

Alice, however, knows what she likes. When her turn comes around back into the book box goes our much loved gutsy, naughty, rather scruffy little princess and out comes the small, neat Ladybird fairy tale, in all its traditional glory. Despite all our attempts at subterfuge and persuasion – from reading to her on her own just before group story-time to making it the least obvious book in the book box – Alice sticks to her choice and of course we respect that.

As you can probably guess, Alice's all-time favourite is Snow White, and as the story begins she loses herself in the make-believe world of fairy-tale land. It is stated in all the textbooks that children with autism lack imagination. I would question this view, as I have seen children deeply absorbed in play that has an imaginative element to it, but I would qualify this by saying that the quality of that play is not the same as the play of most boys and girls of similar ages, often incorporating an autistic child's unique take on life.

I think it is fair to say that Alice plays at being a princess differently to other little girls. Where they might listen to a story then go away and develop elaborate dramas of their own, Alice, on hearing Snow White, for example, becomes that particular Snow White as represented by that particular story version. Rather than listen and then take away the ideas, Alice's language, her facial expressions and her actions exactly mimic those of the Snow White in the storybook. Alice seems to enter into the very essence of the particular storybook princess she is listening to at the time.

And she becomes that princess with all the skill of an Oscar winning actress. Sometimes we wonder at her ability to feel the emotions so intensely and worry that she might never recover from the poisoned apple, without a real Prince Charming to wake her up. But she does and just like in the fairy tale lives happily ever after.

Watching Alice become Snow White as she listens to the story will challenge even the most convinced theorist to modify their view. Whilst Alice is not imagining her own version of Snow White, rather she 'becomes' Snow White as she mirrors exactly the unfolding story, we too suspend our belief and see the princess in her. For us too, as the story unfolds, Alice is no longer our plain, plump little schoolgirl with learning difficulties. She is a beautiful little princess – albeit one who has around her a court of restless, cross and disenchanted courtiers all pretty much indifferent as to whether or not Alice is to get her very own Prince Charming.

The reason I am cautious about accepting that Alice has no imagination rests not only on what could be argued to be merely copying of a story and pictures – although it is difficult to explain how she could be so emotionally involved in that copying if her imagination was not in some way engaging with the unfolding drama of the story – but also because she does occasionally attempt to rope her classmates into joining in her fantasy. Alice knows that a princess wears beautiful clothes, has exquisite dancing shoes and always gets to kiss the most handsome man in the kingdom. Alice knows all these things. And occasionally, without a book to follow, Alice transforms herself into a princess, tossing back her imaginary flowing locks and pointing her dancing shoes in readiness for her last dance with her very own Prince Charming.

Unfortunately for Alice, in our little class, the choice of Prince Charming is limited, not least because most of the children *do* conform to the texts and will have nothing to do with make-believe. Alice for her part would not dream of trying to take Joss away from his beloved train track, or Nathan away from his comic in the corner, but sometimes she is able to find her Prince Charming. Toby, good-natured, bouncy, ever smiling, finds himself held firmly around the waist and whisked around the classroom, which has transformed itself into a ballroom in Alice's mind. (I'm not quite sure what Toby makes of it all, but he gallantly dances along, enjoying the attention.) So, for a few priceless moments Alice and Toby waltz around the classroom, looking for all the world more like a Derby and Joan couple trying to recapture their youth than the happy-ever-after-couple of fairy-tale land, lost in their own private fantasy.

★ ★ ★

Alice is fortunate in having good communication skills. We can often reason and explain things to Alice, and she in turn can ask questions about things she does not understand. Just as I was initially surprised that Alice was in the class, some visitors to the class questioned why such an apparently well-spoken, confident girl needs the extra help a class like ours offers. In many ways it was true that Alice could have fitted in to a mainstream class, as her learning difficulties were moderate and her language skills good. But Alice has many profound difficulties that emerge only when the supportive ambience of her little class disappears and she is faced with the less structured, less supportive environment of the wider world. Then, problems of social understanding, of literal interpretation of words and difficulties with interaction become painfully evident.

It is agreed that Alice will benefit from some integration with a mainstream classroom, enabling her to experience a richer language environment and providing her with valuable social experiences. She goes for an afternoon a week with Erin to support her, and joins a class of five- to six-year-olds. Here, in a bustling classroom, she sits at a table with six unfamiliar children and attempts to join in. She is generally able to do the work (better than some) but she relies heavily on Erin. The chatter and movement of the other children confuses and disorientates Alice. Without Erin by her side to reassure and help her she would flounder. While she tries hard to be part of the group (with Erin skilfully ensuring that the other children include her in their conversation), Alice's lack of understanding of the natural give and take of conversation means it is difficult for her to keep up with these exchanges. She laughs when others laugh, although she has not got the joke, then laughs inappropriately because she thinks that is what is expected of her. She has to work hard, and be constantly encouraged by Erin, in order to stay afloat in this sea of activity that is her group table. Amidst their easy chitchat, Alice's difficulties show up in sharp relief. Whereas in our class of seven she is one of the most attentive and reliable, here the hubbub of classroom life is almost overwhelming her. Her senses become overloaded. She can't concentrate on her work but neither can she join in the fast, furious conversation, with its accompanying subtle nuances of social exchange that mean nothing to her. She lacks the guile of the naughty ones and the concentration of the hard workers. Gently, Erin acts as interpreter, prompt and voice for Alice as she tries to steer her through the social milieu of primary school classroom life.

At playtime, her difficulties become more acute. The vastness of a play-ground teaming with bodies and noise is quite overwhelming. Again, without Erin here to provide a safe anchor of familiarity Alice would be very much out of her depth. The confidence that she displays in our small yard with children who are happy to do their own thing is replaced with trepidation. It becomes clear that this may not be the most helpful way to broaden Alice's educational experiences, and in time she stops going to the school.

I think it is difficult for anyone, even adults with all their social know how, to join an established group and join in confidently, but Alice's difficul-ties are more profound than the issue of confidence alone. The sheer stress of trying to manage all the social skills needed to be part of mainstream class-room life means Alice is functioning in a state of anxiety, even with the support of a well-qualified adult. Her difficulties, which are masked to a degree by the supportive environment of her little class, come to the fore in the larger, more robust environment of a busy primary school class.

When Sam joins our class the opportunity arises to try a different form of integration. Forestpark is a primary school for children with moderate learning difficulties. It has much smaller classes than the mainstream school that Alice has found so challenging. We discuss with the staff the possibility of setting up some integration between the two schools. They feel it will be a valuable experience for their pupils. We are keen to explore a different model of integration. We know, from previous experience, that it is not easy for our pupils to take on board all the stresses of being the newcomer in an estab-lished group. We are anxious to maximise the chances of success. We arrange for a small group of pupils from this neighbouring school to join a mixed class of pupils from our school. This arrangement means that our pupils do not have to deal with the additional stress of being the outsiders. This proves to be a success, as our pupils are more confident with the newcomers on their home ground. Our aim is primarily to encourage friendships and self-esteem. For the pupils from Forestpark their self-esteem is enhanced because for the first time they are the more able; for our pupils these children are their visitors, which give them an enhanced sense of importance. There is overall a very positive feel to these sessions. Sharing activities, tentative friendships emerge and both Sam and Alice benefit from widening the circle of friends that they can talk to. In time, Sam and Alice visit the other school, and because they already know some of the children they are much more confident about dealing with the change of setting. Consequently they are able to gain some valuable social experiences from these exchanges.

But, inevitably (or so it seems), financial pressures from the education authority make it impossible for us to keep this arrangement going. There is a major reorganisation of schools, and Forestpark is relocated. In these changed circumstances it is not possible to arrange the necessary transport and staff to continue such a small-scale programme, however valuable it has proved to be. Despite the positive experience the whole thing comes to an end. This is very frustrating, as I feel it has proved its value in offering both our pupils and those from Forestpark valuable social and emotional experiences that reach to the very core of the pupils' difficulties. It is frustrating as practitioners that economics, rather than good educational practice, determines the course of this particular provision for these pupils.

Back in the classroom, Alice finds her niche. Like so many little girls, she loves to draw pictures. Alice comes into the class in the morning and in the free time whilst we wait for everyone to arrive and unwind from their various journeys into school, settles down with paper and crayons and creates her own versions of princesses. Not only can Alice take on the persona of a fairy-tale princess but she can draw them with such an astounding flair for movement you can practically see them dancing towards their prince. She captures beautifully the way a princess holds out her long, flowing gown just so: the way she tilts her head in a slightly disdainful but oh so regal manner, the way her pretty dancing shoes are delicately poised, waiting for the music to start, even the flutter of her eyelids towards the awaiting and oh so handsome Prince Charming. To me this is further evidence of Alice's ability to use her imagination and bring her original flair and understanding to produce her own story-board images of that fantasy world of the princess that she shares with so many of her contemporaries.

Alice's skill at drawing not only princesses but also people in general shows a talent and an eye for detail that belies her youth. Whenever we have a visitor (and some days it feels as if we have a constant stream of them) Alice captures their image with remarkable accuracy, taking in not only the hair colour, hairstyle, clothes, and shoes they are wearing but also their 'essence'. Visitors can be anything from genuinely friendly and interested in the children to aloof, embarrassed, domineering, patronising, indifferent, timid – a whole range of responses, depending on their reason for visiting and their natural persona. Somehow Alice can pick up on the nervous mother; the arrogant educational psychologist; the enthusiastic student; the severe doctor, and with a few strokes of her pencil she reproduces her impression of them. We always look forward to Alice's artistic summing up of the people who pass through our door. Occasionally we ask her to draw us, to see how she perceives us. I say occasionally because, depending where you stand in Alice's favours at any given time, the results can be far from flattering!

Although children with autism are said to be unaware of other people's feelings, in one very awkward and difficult respect Alice is acutely aware of the embarrassment she can cause in certain social settings. In the classroom it is not too bad. Safety in numbers and a sense of humour mean that we can deal with her outbursts with the nonchalant indifference good behaviour management dictates. But in public, it is different. Having a little girl scream at the top of her voice 'Leave me alone! You are breaking my arm!' is guaranteed to draw unfavourable attention.

Somehow, in her short life, Alice has picked up on the fact that if she screams at the top of her voice that she is being attacked and hurt, then she is likely to get what she wants. So whenever she is disgruntled about something, she cries out. She has a very dramatic and convincing manner. Whatever her understanding of its effects, Alice is quite prepared to use this approach whenever the need arises. Like any little girl, the need arises when she is not getting her own way. Whilst she uses her dramatic cries sparingly she chooses her moments well – in supermarkets, swimming pools, on walks to the local shops and, of course, when we have visitors.

Understanding that this is Alice's way of registering her protest is one thing; being on the receiving end of such cries of abuse towards her person is something else. When we are out as a class and Alice decides, for example, that she does not want to get back on the bus, she cries out 'Oh no! My fingers are broken!' and begins to sob. It is embarrassing for us, of course. If a member of the public were to take her cries seriously, we could find ourselves in an awkward position. But no one ever challenges us. It begins to worry us that no one so much as questions us during these dramatic incidents. We do attract plenty of stares. Alice is very convincing. She will turn bright red. Her voice will have a real edge to it. Her reputation (at home and at school) as a drama queen is well deserved. But no member of the public ever does more than look on from a distance.

I hope it is because people see that we are clearly from a school, that we are obviously kind women looking after difficult children. Even so, we would feel happier if someone would at least take the time to come over and talk to us to confirm that we are, indeed, bona fide carers. Working with such vulnerable children, we are always conscious of how easily their safety can be compromised. It would be reassuring to know that the majority of people won't pass by without comment if a major commotion happens suggesting someone is apparently trying to harm a child. With the terrible consequences an indifferent public had on the horrific murder of James Bulger, for example, we all agree that we would feel happier if someone, at least once, took the time to double check that everything is all right for Alice.

It is worrying for us all that Alice seems unable to tone down her over-dramatic expressions of displeasure. It is very important for Alice to learn a more acceptable way of expressing herself. Her mother is understandably concerned that it might become like the boy who cried 'Wolf' so often, that when he genuinely needed everyone to believe him, no one does.

We develop strategies to help Alice behave more appropriately. We talk to Alice about the need to be truthful. We give her more appropriate phrases to use: 'No, I don't want to' rather than 'You are killing me'.

We demonstrate dramatic exclamations of displeasure that we hope will be more attractive to her: 'Oh bother!', 'Fiddlesticks!' She listens and nods her agreement and tries out the phrases while happily going about her business. Then at the slightest provocation she lets out her blood-curdling cry! 'Stop killing me!' Reasoning in the midst of this emotional state is utterly futile. She interrupts any attempts at calming her with further screams of protest. 'My ears are breaking!'

Then we remember how much Alice longs to be a princess. 'Oh, Alice,' we exclaim in exaggerated disbelief. 'A princess would never behave like that!' Alice adjusts her whole demeanour. She straightens her shoulders. She lifts her head, shaking her hair in disdain. In a voice as haughty as she imagines a disgruntled princess might muster in such circumstances she declares, 'Well, I'm very sorry but I just don't want to do that!'

We realise we have hit on something here. It becomes increasingly clear that reminding Alice of how a princess might behave is the best way into teaching her more appropriate behaviour. We have to take care not to abuse and over-use this knowledge, but there is no doubting its usefulness in helping her through this difficult phase. As her whole manner changes and she becomes a sugary sweet, goody two-shoes kind of princess she forgets her tantrum and becomes our plump little girl trying hard to grow up and learn to be a proper princess.

Occasionally though, like any little princess, she has her moments and no amount of persuasion will make her change her dramatic screams. 'Get off me!' she admonishes in a far from regal voice. 'I'm *not* a princess. I'm an Alice! And I'm very cross!' But then in the telling some of her anger diffuses. As we hug her and settle her back down the loud, compromising dramatic screaming becomes a more childish moan and our little girl becomes the little girl she is, doing her best to make sense of our far from make-believe world.

Alice's mum discusses Alice's challenging behaviour and how she came to understand more about her daughter's autism

"She settled down, but we had our tantrums. Didn't want to go, sometimes. Didn't want to get on the bus. And then, sometimes, didn't want to get off the bus to come home…flinging herself on the floor if she didn't want to do something. Yes, if she didn't want to go anywhere or do something she'd throw herself on the floor and scream. You just had to walk away from her and ignore her, because if you turned around and said 'Stop being silly' or something, it would make her worse. Yes, she'd do it in public. When you took her into the toilets [she'd shout] 'Get off my knickers!' And when you come out of the toilet you were so embarrassed! People were looking at you, thinking 'what were you doing to her in there?' It was so uncomfortable.

Well, when she was diagnosed I was told she would never settle down; she would never make friends with anyone; she would never do anything. Just be a lonely little child who would sit in the corner and wouldn't interact with anyone. But when she went to school she started to interact with other people and make friends...I thought she'd just be a, well, live in her own little world but she didn't. She started interacting with other people, which surprised me. From then on I just took it from day to day, what she was doing. Well, about six months after she started school, since she started there, she came on brilliant...

When I saw her at school, she was totally different. She was very quiet at home, but when she was at school she would go out to play and she wouldn't stick to you. When she was at home, she'd stay with me. She wouldn't let me out of her sight. But when she was at school and I was there with her, or in the classroom with her, she'd be off playing. She wasn't bothered about me, where I was, whether I'd gone or stayed. She was totally different. But at home you had to leave the door open, when I was cooking, so she could see me. Yes, I was put out. 'Oh, she's leaving me!' But in another sense, she has to stand on her own two feet. It's what she has to do. [Tears] When she was at school she loved school, when she got into school she really liked it. I suppose you had a lot of trouble with her at school...

When she was little she used to go up to people and talk to them. She used to talk to anybody. Really frightening, that. You couldn't let her out of your sight in case she talked to someone, a stranger. You couldn't take your eyes off her...I think she has learnt through school and the process of growing up...the school has done a lot for her.

What I was told originally was, well it was quite frightening. To be told that this child is going to be dependent on me for the rest of my life, for the rest of their life. What do I do? Well, what does she do when I'm not here? Who's going to look after her? But she's totally changed. It's just totally changed... I know now that she could survive in the outside, that she could cope. But then, I thought she'd never be able to go out on her own, speak to anybody, and be safe. But now it seems to have sort of drifted to one minute she was a little girl that couldn't do anything for herself and now she's a little girl, well a teenager that can do practically everything that she can put her mind to...it's a gradual thing...

She used to be such a dramatic performer. She's not such a performer any more but when she was younger...it was quite embarrassing for [her uncle]. She'd go 'You are breaking my arm!' or 'Let go of my fingers. You are breaking them!'

It was very embarrassing for him in front of people, but he had to overcome that. He just switched off and concentrated on what he was doing, what she was doing. People just don't understand.

I think now, with all the publicity about autism, people understand ... because with school trips now with the little ones they are just about the same age as Alice was when she was dramatic, people just see to go by and not look twice, but when Alice was little people used to stand and stare at you and 'Well, get this child off the floor!' but they don't now. You felt like you had to explain to people why she was behaving like that. And if you didn't explain to people why she was behaving like that, they'd think, you know, you are a bad mother. You can't control your child and you think 'What do I do?' It put you in a horrible position. I'm thinking, 'Am I? Am I doing something wrong?' I'd had no [idea about autism]. When they said [she has autism] and I said 'Well, what will Alice be able to do?', they just said 'Well, no, she won't be able to do this and she won't be able to do that'...

It was much better being able to talk to people about little things. Other parents. They would have the same problem and I'd think, well I'm not doing this wrong. Because you weren't getting the information from doctors, health visitors. People like that would say, 'Well, we don't know much about it.' But the school knew, well, a bit about it [laugh]. But you knew more than what I did and I think as time has gone by everybody has helped each other and that's what everybody wanted. And if you didn't have the answer at school, you could go somewhere else. The autistic society would answer your questions...

It was important, meeting other parents, talking to all the other teachers and seeing older children and how they were progressing through the school. Well, seeing there is life ahead. Before, I thought there was nothing to look forward to. But when you seen the other children in the school doing their own thing, walking about without being supervised...I thought I'd never see Alice at [that level of independence]. I'd been told that she'd never amount to anything really. Which was horrible, it was really horrible to think about at the time. Really depressing. When she'd had a tantrum, you'd think 'Oh I wish I could send her back' but then the next minute she'd say something like 'I love you mummy' and you'd think 'Oooh'.

The first year after being diagnosed – she wasn't diagnosed until she was five – she'd already been at the school, before then I didn't know what was the matter with her. I thought she was just deaf. I thought she was badly behaved. Then when we got the diagnosis...it was devastating. But also, I didn't know what it was, what it entailed. So when they said she'd just be sitting in a corner in her own little world I thought, you know, what have I let myself in for? When the doctor said it was autism well, what is it? It just took a long time for it to sink in to what it was. I started asking questions and people said 'I don't know'.

I went into the school and talked to other parents and they said yes, this is what they do, this is what they can do. From there I just thought I had to see how things go. Live day-to-day, week-to-week. And that's what I did.

Well, you know, I wanted her to be normal, to treat her normally. But you couldn't. You had to bend the rules a bit. I hoped it would just disappear. She had friends and she'd play rough and they wouldn't come any more. That made it worse really. She wouldn't be asked to parties. She'd race round and be rough. She'd only go to parties from school, because they knew what she'd be like. I only had the mums from the school.

She's not a horrible little child any more, she's more of a friend to you. Before she used to be demanding. This little tiny two-year-old, demanding all the time. You couldn't have a minute to yourself. If I knew everything I know now, I would probably have done lots of things differently. I'd know what I was comparing with. I didn't know what I was doing. I didn't know where to turn. But now, parents have got lots of information from everywhere about what the child can achieve and the worst scenario.

I did feel very angry when she was first diagnosed. But as the years have gone by it has just got easier. It's just having someone to talk to who knows what you are talking about. [If I were to talk to a new parent now I would say] 'Life begins now and it gets better.'

I've spoken to some of the parents of the little ones now and they say there's nothing to look forward to and I say 'Yes there is. I've got a daughter who couldn't speak, who used to misbehave all the time and look at her now.'

You can't understand that this child, from a misbehaving, screaming [child] can be sitting down reading a book quietly. Gives people hope… I thought she wouldn't be able to sit down and learn to read. She'd be off doing something else or running round, because that's what she used to do, running round.

But yes, that's what she used to do. She'd sit down and read a book to you. You'd sit there amazed. She'd read straight through the book.

'Right, finished. I'll read something else.'

'Well, later.'

And then she'd remember later, well we haven't read this book yet.

'Well, bedtime now, too late.'

'Read it tomorrow then?'

'Okay.'

And then she'd remember we hadn't read the book, so we'd read another book, a Ladybird book off the shelf. She amazed me. I think she surprised everybody."

Chapter 3

The Philosopher

Nathan is small, pale and vulnerable looking. He has no discernible verbal communication skills beyond a very quiet and rare 'yes' or 'no'. He does not seek out physical contact and is often found watching the goings-on around him from a safe distance. He loves books about things and dinosaurs. He has an infectious laugh and a stubborn streak.

The little boy in the newspaper photo peers out at me from the safety of his dustbin. I instantly recognise Nathan, although the boy in the photo is called Tom and the article is about his life at home, highlighting for the reader some of his bizarre and incomprehensible behaviours, one of which is to hide in dustbins. To the best of my knowledge Nathan has never hidden in a dustbin but it is easy to believe he would, like the little boy in the picture. His body language shows that hiding is preferable to not hiding, even in a dustbin.

Perhaps more than anyone else in my little class of unique and complex children Nathan epitomises all the popular understanding of autism. He rarely speaks. When he does his voice seems to come from the very depths of his soul to be caught on the wind like a wisp of thin white cloud, no sooner spoken than lost in the vastness of the skies. He is insular, guarding his own space, complete in his own company, deep in his own thoughts. Insular is probably not the best word. I sense that he is a very private person. He seems to be as deep as the darkest well and as unfathomable as the vast oceans. He holds himself apart. It is as if he is a hermit contemplating the mysteries of life, yet lacking the protection of a hermitage.

Nathan has an aura of vulnerability about him. Instinctively you want to protect him. But he has no time for sentimentality. His apparent fragility masks a determined character. He cannot be cajoled. If he wants to do something he does it. When he doesn't see the point in something, or he disagrees with you, he lets you know in no uncertain terms. He watches the world from a distance with a steady gaze, diverted only when someone tries to break into his concentration. It is only by watching closely that you realise Nathan is taking things in, his quick, indifferent glances towards something that interests him giving you the faintest hint that he might just be persuaded to join in.

Although he is a slight dot of a boy, light as a feather to pick up, he is very tough physically. He hates to be touched, except on his own terms. In self-defence he can writhe and squirm and wriggle like the slippiest of eels, working himself into a whirling dervish, with superhuman powers to repel any contact, however well meant.

Nathan comes and goes silently. He enters the classroom with Moya, his escort, passively, wordlessly, obediently holding her hand from taxi to classroom door. Here he will equally passively let go the hand and slip out of his oversized blue anorak quickly and unaided, then take himself solemnly off to a quiet corner to hide behind a large book. From there he will occasionally look up to observe the antics of his classmates.

If he reaches the classroom door and he is unhappy, he will sink to his knees, pull in his arms and head and disappear into the big blue tent of his coat leaving only his two little hands visible as he reaches up to pull the collar tight around his small blond head. Under this tent-like look out post he silently lurks. If anyone tries to intrude (coaxing teachers, boisterous Toby) he squeals, writhes and digs himself in deeper, wrapping himself into a ball of blue nothingness, his coat protecting him as effectively as the hard shell of a tortoise protects its soft vulnerable body.

When he senses danger might be over he cautiously emerges from a chink in the collar opening. Two deep blue brooding eyes quizzically scan the horizon. Like a submarine telescope checking for mines, Nathan assesses whether it might be safe to expose himself to the perils of the classroom. Coast clear, his head emerges, still cautiously sweeping the near horizon for the slightest signs of danger, ready to disappear back into his shell if anything threatening approaches. All being well, he continues to emerge, until, exposed and vulnerable, he is ready to take on the challenges of a day at school.

Nathan speaks in a soft, far-away voice using little more than a functional 'yes' or 'no' in response to questions. This paucity of language adds to his self-inflicted isolation and enhances the impression of a little lost boy. He speaks with all the gravitas of a politician and the gentleness of a mother soothing her baby. In these two little words he holds the whole world in a delicate balance, poised between calm and chaos.

This vulnerability transforms itself at a stroke when something upsets his equilibrium. He erupts into a whirling dervish, furious and frantic to keep all at bay as he expresses his utter frustration and distress at whoever or whatever has upskittled the delicate balance of his private little world. These outbursts of dismay are frequent and furious. They are also distressing to all concerned as they so often seem to appear out of nowhere and disappear long before any understanding of their cause is found. Witnessing such an isolated display of distress from such a small, vulnerable boy is upsetting in the extreme. It is as if this child is some kind of changeling – one moment a vulnerable little boy, the next a self-possessed raging sprite. Because it is difficult to know the cause of all his outbursts, there is a sense of treading on eggshells around him. After all, no one wants to be the trigger for such an upset, but sometimes without knowing why, you can become exactly that.

Dealing with such unpredictable behaviour is challenging. It is not possible to come up with easy solutions and quick fixes. Often, the best course of action is observation and monitoring. Looking for specific triggers is a useful tool in addressing challenging behaviour. Sometimes it is possible to trace the cause of an outburst to an easily remedied cause and steps can then be taken to minimise the effects. For example, it may be that a cupboard door is slightly ajar or a picture on the wall is flapping. It may be a word that upsets. At one point Nathan became distraught every time Lotti said 'seventeen' over and over. Incidents that are triggered by another child can be particularly difficult to manage, as it is often a case of one child's obsession pitted against another's apparently irrational response. Without understanding what is going on in Nathan's mind it is not always possible to avert these outbursts of frustration and anger. Then it is necessary to provide a safe environment for him to work out his feelings and manage his behaviour himself. Life is not easy for Nathan. There are many times when his world collides head on with our world.

Sometimes, however, the reasons are clear and they are to do with being part of a community and learning to take turns, make changes, conform to rules, be part of a group. He doesn't want to stop looking at a particular book. His favourite food is not on offer. He doesn't like the song we are singing. He does not want to take off his coat. He doesn't want Toby to say hello to him. Our job then is to help him as much as possible to learn to understand and handle the complexities of living in a social world and to help him find ways of developing to his full potential.

But Nathan is a dark horse. He guards what he knows and what he can do and is reluctant to let on. For example, he looks at books but no one knew he could read for some time. How he learnt to read is debatable. It appears that he taught himself. Initially he resists any attempts to try and teach him to read; he doesn't even tolerate sharing a book with anyone else; he doesn't want to sit next to you; he doesn't want to talk out loud.

It is only when the structure of the reading session makes him feel safe enough that he lets us know, in his quiet little voice, whispering staccato words from increasingly difficult texts, never stumbling, never rushing, never showing off, that we realise that he has been doing more than looking at the pictures in the books he hid behind all this time. He still does not answer questions about what he is reading aloud (in his barely audible whisper) so it has

been impossible to assess his level of understanding, but he does have favourite books and responds to stories with intense interest and occasional
laughter. When reading aloud, however, he appears to be excruciatingly
embarrassed. So it is a testament to his bravery and perhaps to his trust in us
that he has opened up enough to let us know that he knows more than we
thought he knew. Whenever Nathan shares a private part of his skills with you
it feels like a great privilege. You can't help wondering what it has cost him to
open up a chink in his private world and share it with someone else.

Settling to work is not one of Nathan's strengths, particularly when the
work is unfamiliar. Like Sam, failure is not in Nathan's vocabulary. He cannot
tolerate the possibility of making mistakes. Often, before he settles to his
work, he sidles up to the work table, surreptitiously checking out what is on
offer. If he feels confident about the work he will settle down to do the task. If,
however, he feels in any way challenged by the work, he does everything in
his power to avoid it. This can range from keeping well away from the table
through to a major tantrum, depending on his mood and, probably, ours. He
will leap away from us, writhing and wriggling on the floor, lodging himself
firmly in a tight corner resisting any attempts to get near him.

Once he is upset there is no placating him. Any physical contact sends him
demented. Any verbal contact has the same effect. It is impossible to do
anything with him or for him in this state. We have to wait for him to calm
down, unfurl and return to whatever has upset him in his own time. Or not.
For Nathan is very much his own man. He decides whether he thinks joining
in is worthwhile. If it is, fine. He will sit – not always in the group – he prefers
to be on the periphery and observe from a safe distance, taking everything in
quietly, unobtrusively, secretly. And if he doesn't want to do something, he
will resist any attempts to be cajoled. Nathan does not do bribes. He does not
do promises. He either does. Or doesn't.

Teaching Nathan new skills and knowledge is understandably difficult
under these circumstances, but they are no more than the day-to-day challenge of working with children with autism and we learn ways of meeting
these challenges. Nathan responds well to praise and loves to be told he is a
'clever boy'. Despite his nonchalant shrug, his shoulders straighten and he
walks that bit taller when he hears those words.

Nathan is quite competent at many activities – he enjoys many produc-
tive, calm, self-esteem building sessions where he is confident enough to rise
to the challenge. But if he suspects that he might not get things right, he is off.
Mistakes are agonies Nathan is not prepared to endure. He avoids the possibil-

ity of making mistakes at all cost. Once he associates an activity with failure he regards it with deep distrust ever after.

With patience and a certain amount of cunning – like slipping in the odd snippet of knowledge amongst a load of easy to achieve tasks – Nathan is able to tolerate learning some new skills. These new ideas, skills and knowledge are carefully sandwiched between easy, familiar work, to sweeten the pill. But even when he is apparently taking no notice, Nathan is often watching and listening from the sidelines. This way he is able to absorb new experiences within the privacy of his own mind. As with reading, we see occasional evidence that Nathan has learnt a new skill or mastered an unfamiliar concept despite his refusal to conform to our conventional teaching methods.

While his tantrums can be wild and furious he does have a degree of control about them. He never hurts himself or others. He just makes himself unapproachable. But then, as if from nowhere, Nathan begins to bang his head. It is an easy thing to write but it is a distressing thing to watch. He finds a hard surface, like the floor or the edge of a table, and bangs his head down. He rarely makes a sound, although it must be very painful. Then, within a horribly short space of time, Nathan takes to banging his head at the slightest provocation – a look cast in his direction at the wrong moment, a biscuit offered when it was not wanted – and we have spiralled into one of the most difficult and distressing of behaviour management situations to face as a teacher.

Self-harming is a heartbreaking thing to observe and an enormously difficult behaviour to manage and help. As a teacher you go through all kinds of emotions from guilt to grief to helplessness, all the while watching helplessly as you fail to prevent a small, vulnerable boy from causing increasing bruising and distress to himself.

It is the bleakest of times for us, and one that is very painful to recall. Watching a little boy consistently and deliberately beat his head against any hard surface at the slightest provocation, and finding that in trying to help we only exacerbate the situation, is a very disturbing experience. Collectively we feel a huge wave of guilt and despair that we are unable to prevent this destructive self-harming from happening. Every attempt to help is met with further head banging and such is the power of this behaviour that slowly Nathan's ability to join in with anything, to be happy at any activity, begins to close in on him. He understands the power of this behaviour to keep at bay any of the impositions our difficult world demands of him. We see him gradually losing himself into this closed-down world of increasingly narrow opportunity for happiness.

This is not the place (nor do I have the expertise) to discuss the possible reasons for self-harming and the best ways to deal with it (see Appendix 2). We seek advice and discuss the best way forward. In consultation with Nathan's parents he is issued with a special helmet to protect him from further injury. This gives us the necessary opportunity to help him modify his behaviour without provoking further self-injury. A behaviour programme is put in place. He is allowed to take home a favourite book as a reward for self-control. Gradually the frequency of his self-harming diminishes. Nathan's rage at himself, us, the world, subsides. Eventually his behaviour settles back into more manageable tantrums and the bruising on his forehead dies down. He still bangs his head, but gently now, as if to remind us that he can and will resume head banging if things get too much ever again.

Thankfully, the episode is relatively short-lived, but even now, although the parents were fully consulted and supportive of the intervention and help given to Nathan, it is a period of his life that they would rather not talk about. I understand this fully. In writing about this time it brings back a mix of emotions and thoughts about the complexities of the autistic mind. There are so many unanswered questions, as there are for so much behaviour we encounter amongst these children that shows up the paucity of our understanding of autism. As a team, we all felt deskilled and vulnerable during this time, and it reminded us starkly of the weight of responsibility facing us in looking after these children. It also brought us together as a team. Having others around to support in such an emotionally fraught time shows up the strengths of teamwork. Working together towards such an important goal is very rewarding. With our different personalities we were able to keep working towards our goal, picking each other up when we became disheartened, encouraging one another and sharing the emotional fall-out.

For me, working with Nathan provides one of the starkest reminders that we have barely scraped the surface of our understanding of autism and, more importantly, of communication between people who have a seemingly totally different worldview. One analogy often drawn on is that we are from different planets, and certainly there are times when it feels that might be so.

An incident with Nathan makes me question just how many of the difficulties that are encountered between the autistic and non-autistic worlds are a
result of a different way of communicating about the shared world we live in.
By sheer luck, a moment of fortunate inspiration or some other fluke of fate,
one day I perform a little miracle and make Nathan a very happy boy. I give
him a small, lined exercise book and write his timetable in it.

The miracle is that neither of us has a clue how we reach the point of
understanding that possessing this exercise book is the one thing that Nathan
desperately desires. From going with Nathan to the store cupboard to get the
exercise book to returning hand-in-hand, happy, relaxed and expectant back
to the classroom Nathan has changed from an angry, frustrated, uncooperative
pupil into a chuffed-to-pieces six-year-old who seems to have grown an extra
two inches, so puffed up with pride is he at this development in his perceived
status in his little class of 'non-communicating children' as the Unit was so
hideously called. And to give him this happiness has been a fortuitous stab of
desperate lateral thinking on my part. And probably a perfectly logical, clear
communication on Nathan's. Let me explain.

All the children have individual timetables. They are there to support their
understanding of their day at school. The visual reference is necessary to alle-
viate and explain in an understandable way what to expect from the school
day, from the time the children enter the class, until the time they go home. It
cuts down on anxiety, tantrums and panic attacks common to children with
autism when they are unable to access a clear picture of what is going on
around them. Times of transition from one activity to another can cause
enormous problems for someone with autism. Coping with change is not one
of their strong points. The visual reference of these timetables helps the
children hold on to facts in a way that is meaningful. Activities are represented
by pic-symbols – black and white images of activities or objects related to
events. We use them as a means of communication for the majority of children,
although for Lotti even these were too obscure to be helpful. Sam and Alice
are competent readers and so each has a written timetable. These are considerably easier for staff to set out, as the pic-symbol timetables involve searching
for a variety of pictures amongst a whole array of images kept in a large box
file. This box file contains a huge range of pic-symbols, from those in common
daily use, such as play, PE, dinner, free choice, writing, number, painting,
sand, water, story, singing, bus and home, to rarely used ones like hospital.
'Free choice time' for example is represented by a child playing with bricks;
playtime by children running; dinner by a dinner tray; toilet by a picture of a

toilet and so on. Some are taken from a commercially produced scheme and some are home made. So in the box file we have a variety of pic-symbols we have yet to find a use for.

Each evening, in preparation for the next day, we fill five timetables with an array of pic-symbols and each morning the children come in and check their timetables, scanning them to see whether the day takes their fancy or not. The fact that every child does this check unprompted, as soon as they start their school day, demonstrates the value that these communication aids have for the children. Even those with good communication skills are more reassured by the written timetable than by any amount of verbal explanation.

Knowing what happens and, more important, what happens next, reduces a lot of anxiety for the children. This is perfectly reasonable. We all like to know what is happening with our day, and unconsciously have a number of routines and prompts that help us feel comfortable. Little children at school like to know what they are up to and if today has their favourite activity in it. They will ask each other, their parents and their teacher and adjust their feelings about the day according to what lies in store for them. The difference with our little class is that talking is not enough, even for the most articulate. A visual representation of the day is a crucial tool for helping towards a better understanding of their complex world.

Of course, as with any child, that is not to say that because it is on the timetable it is welcome and, like all children, ours have their favourite activities and those they would like to avoid at all costs. They are just as likely to moan, complain and try to avoid an activity that doesn't suit as any other child. The difference in our class is just how that moaning is expressed – from disappearing for long intervals into the toilet to lying on the floor having the screaming ab-dabs. This is all part of the school day and the challenge of the job.

When Nathan begins being awkward in the middle of his number work with Sally, and throws the work on the floor, jumps on his chair and starts screaming, Sally takes it all in her stride. Number work is not one of Nathan's favourite activities and he often kicks off about it, although usually once settled to it he continues, albeit in bad grace, to the end. Sally picks up the unifix that are scattered on the floor. She shows Nathan his timetable that shows 'number work' followed by 'free choice' and reiterates verbally as she is doing so that when he has finished it will be his free choice time. This often helps to resettle a child. She opens the exercise book at the appropriate page and tries to continue.

Nathan, still squealing and bouncing on his chair, writes 'cut' in the exercise book. He should have been writing a number, as the lesson is about 'consolidating and recording numbers 5–10'. But he writes 'cut'. Despite her best efforts, nothing can persuade Nathan to continue with the number work. But he is not, unusually, trying to get away from the table. He writes 'cut' again, under the first 'cut'. Used to dealing with the unknown and the strange, and realising that somehow this is important to him, Sally reads the word back to him and waits expectantly. No response. So again she draws his attention back to his timetable pic-symbols, hoping that this might settle him. 'Look Nathan, number, then free choice.'

Nathan responds by squealing even louder, banging his head on the table and writing 'cut', under the previous two 'cut' words. Sally calls for support. Sometimes (not often, but sometimes) one of us instantly knows what might be going on when a child gets inextricably but obviously frustrated, as Nathan clearly is. It is not unusual for a child to get extremely cross over something we do not understand, only to find that the same thing happened yesterday, when working with someone else and they discovered the cause. For example, Joss became tearful one day while working with Sally. Once he found a red pencil to work with, instead of the blue one, he was fine. The next day, working with Erin, he becomes tearful again. Sally is able to suggest trying him with a red pencil and sure enough the tears stop. Suddenly red pencils have taken an important place in Joss's working style even though up to that point he had shown no preference for the colour of his pencil at all. Perhaps Nathan has developed a foible that either Erin or I know about. So, did either of us know what might be bothering him? No. We can't recall any particular quirks affecting his work at the present.

Impatient with us Nathan takes the law into his own hands, so to speak, and goes to the classroom cupboard. Rummaging through the pic-symbols filing system he triumphantly withdraws a pic-symbol of a pair of scissors with 'cut' written below the picture. Satisfied, he returns to the table, puts the pic-symbol on the table and waits, expectantly. Clearly now we will understand.

We don't. We don't use this symbol. It was one of the commercially produced ones that are in the filing system in case it comes in useful, but we have a different symbol for our Design Technology lessons (the official title for our messy gluing and sticking session). It is not a symbol any of us can remember using with Nathan, or any one else.

Does he want scissors? To cut something? Well, he is not going to get any. We have seen the results of many a pupil's haircut following the discovery of scissors, and we are not going to be compliant in any more hatchet jobs. But somehow that doesn't seem to be it. After all, the scissors are kept in an adjoining room and surely if Nathan wants them he would have tried to get at them. It's not as if he usually stands on ceremony. If he wants something, he goes for it. Why the writing the word down? Why is he writing it down like a list?

I don't know to this day why I thought of it, but suddenly I see a pattern, like Sam and Alice's written timetable. Has Nathan decided he wants a written timetable? In the absence of any other idea, under his written 'cut' I write 'number' and under that 'free choice'. Nathan's taut little body relaxes. He reads the words in his tiny far away voice. Excited, I ask him if he wants a written timetable. He doesn't answer. I say 'Let's go and get a timetable book' and hold out my hand. He takes it and we walk hand-in-hand, not speaking, along the corridor to the store cupboard. I hand him a red-covered narrow exercise book, identical to Sam and Alice's written timetable diaries. Immediately he grows two inches taller. His chest puffs out. The faintest hint of a smile flits, momentarily, across his lips. He grasps my hand again and we return to the classroom.

I write. He watches. Not me – the list of words. Satisfied, he practically skips to the worktop where he silently, solemnly, places his treasured timetable next to Sam and Alice's. He ticks off 'number' with his chunky red pencil, reads 'free choice' and skips off to solemnly observe the world from behind a big book. We don't get so much as a backward glance.

Communication is a complex thing. That exchange was pure hit and miss. I have no idea why Nathan chose 'cut' to represent his longing to be like Sam and Alice and have a written timetable, when he could have so easily copied out their timetables, his own timetable, the word timetable, anything directly and obviously connected with the timetables in daily use, regularly, familiarly in the classroom. He could have torn up his timetable, or fetched Alice's from the worktop where they are all laid out. He could have taken Sally by the hand and pulled her to the cupboard and pointed – this is a technique Lotti regularly uses to help you meet her needs, throwing your arm up in the general direction of the biscuit tin or desired object.

I have no idea what would have happened if we had not come to the understanding we did. All I do know is that it is utterly pointless to think we know all there is to know about communication. I wonder, after this bizarre exchange of understanding and misunderstanding (and even now utter bewilderment on my part as to what actually went on), what else I have utterly failed to understand and whether Nathan, or indeed anyone else, is equally bewildered by my own complete failure to communicate sensibly with him.

This is not the only time Nathan challenges us in our understanding of how children with minimal verbal communication and an outward indifference to others might be thinking and communicating. As a teacher, the government is constantly inundating me with new initiatives and dictates about how and what I should be teaching. At one point the flavour of the month is to address the issue of bullying. This causes an enormous amount of discussion amongst our staff as we try to disentangle some of the complex exchanges between our pupils that cause particular distress.

In a later chapter you will meet Toby. Toby's enthusiasm to say 'hello' to everyone causes problems for Nathan for whom it is a kind of torture. Similarly, Nathan is intolerant of Liam's singing and, much to the delight of Liam, Nathan will squeal angrily at Liam when he breaks into a happy rendition of the latest pop song. Both Toby and Liam know the effect they have on Nathan but are unable or unwilling to modify their behaviour. Does this constitute bullying, we wonder? Does a compulsive desire to get a reaction from another pupil mean that child is trying to bully, or do the difficulties of understanding about emotion and social exchange mean that it is essentially impossible to actively bully if you are autistic? We wrestle with these questions, but come to no conclusions.

I dutifully find and read to the class a book about twins starting school, where one is bullied and learns how to deal with it (*Trouble with the Tucker Twins* by Rose Impey). Although it would certainly have been a useful book in a mainstream classroom to initiate debate about bullying, it has absolutely no impact on the children in my class. It is what I have come to call a fidget book – one without rhythmic text, bold pictures, repetition, counting or drama and therefore one that fails to engage my very discerning audience. Not one child has responded to it in any way – it does not have enough shouting, repetition or numbers in it to grab anyone's attention. It sinks without trace into the bottom of the book box. No one chooses it at story-time or looks at it again.

One day, some weeks later, we have a visit from an ex-pupil. He had been the biggest boy in the class, towering over little Nathan, who unhappily found himself occasionally on the receiving end of this lad's rather hefty thump. This thump, like so much 'aggression' from autistic children, was given out as an expression of immense frustration or fear whenever life got too much. It was not, we all agreed, a vindictive attempt to hurt someone. It was a powerful means of communication, one that couldn't be ignored. When Nathan got in the way he was thumped. If we were there first, to protect him, we were thumped. He didn't target a particular person, as sometimes happens. It was just unfortunate if you were the nearest when he was in that mood. But it was not bullying. It was not done in a calm, calculated manner designed to victimise and control someone else. That was our opinion up to this point.

Nathan makes it abundantly clear that it is not how he sees things. When he sees his old classmate, taller and stockier than ever, striding into his old classroom Nathan makes a beeline for the book box. Hastily rummaging through it he grabs a book and dashes out of the classroom to the safety of the corridor. There we find him with the very book that had apparently been an incomprehensibly boring book, when I read it to the class so dutifully weeks earlier. Clearly it had struck a chord with Nathan, although at the time there was no hint that he was even bothering to listen. Now he makes his feelings crystal clear. Whatever we think of this imposing boy's intentions, Nathan is in no doubt that the bully has returned. We let him stay in the corridor, one of us talks quietly to him about bullying, friendship and respect. I trust that he is taking in more than his indifferent air suggests. We are learning fast that we can take nothing for granted with Nathan. It is a lesson in the social intricacies of relationships that we learn from.

Once again it is a salutary reminder that making judgements about understanding, emotional maturity and communication skills relating to a child with autism is a dodgy, inexact and sometimes misleading science. It is another lesson in the dangers of making sweeping statements about the emotional intelligence of these children, who give so little away but sometimes surprise (and shock) us with the depth of their emotional vocabulary.

History should already have taught us that we know far less than we think about autism (and that some of what we thought we knew has been proved to be wrong). Even so, you go into any staff room of teachers of children with autism and you will hear the authoritative exclamation 'Of course, children with autism can't do that!'

It is necessary, indeed vital, to remember that we only know the tip of the iceberg about our selves, let alone about children with a condition as complex and poorly understood as autism. As an example of how quickly perceptions change with understanding, when I started teaching, it was accepted that you could not have books out on general display because 'children with autism don't respect books'.

Our book box is full of well-thumbed books, admittedly some more tatty than they might be in a class of 30 mainstream pupils, but often because they are looked at again, and again, and again. And who are we to say that a child looking at a book upside down is 'not doing it properly'? To see a child go into paroxysms of delight at the bright colours on a page, and want to look at that page day after day after day, makes you sometimes think that perhaps it is you who is missing something here.

Teaching, if done well, is a two-way thing. The teacher should be constantly learning from the pupil. Where this happens that teacher comes away from the experience richer and more thoughtful. Teaching a child with autism can be a most rewarding learning experience, but only if you first recognise that you, the teacher, need to do a lot of the learning.

Whilst Nathan has some difficult days at school, he also has many happy times. And because he is such a quiet spoken, watchful little boy, with such a wise, studious look about him, it is always a great treat to be invited to share things with him. He often keeps his love of books to himself, but when he reads a story to you, or points out some interesting facts – he especially likes books about objects, dinosaurs and vehicles – you know he is sharing more of himself in that act than the casual friendliness of many children.

One of his greatest charms is his sense of humour. When you are let in on the joke you know that Nathan is letting you into his own world and trusting that you will join in on his terms and with his understanding. Of course, a lot of his humour is private and hidden, so that he might inexplicably start to chuckle away to himself, an infectious giggle that lights up his often tense face and makes us all turn to see if we too can share the joke. Usually we have absolutely no idea what has tickled him, but occasionally Nathan shares something with us, like the day he comes in and splutters out joyfully 'Bull in a china shop'.

He collapses into a helpless fit of giggles and we can't help but be caught up in his infectious good-humour. Throughout the day, whenever we want to see Nathan smiling we nudge him and say 'bull in a china shop'. It works every time. He giggles away and we giggle along with him. Likewise he sets us off by announcing 'bull in a china shop' at arbitrary moments – like while he is emptying his tray at dinnertime, or perched on his chair at the end of the day, relaxed and ready for a laugh. 'Bull in a china shop' kept us chuckling all day.

The following day, full of our usual optimism, we greet Nathan merrily at the door with 'bull in a china shop'. With a withering look, Nathan takes off his coat and without a word or a smile he scoots off to a quiet corner where he buries his head in a large book about kitchen appliances. As Toby approaches him with his cheery grin Nathan begins to squeal angrily. Ah well, another day!

Nathan's mum discusses the expectations she had of the school, and her pride in Nathan's achievements

"With him being so young, I didn't know whether he would learn anything or not. I didn't know much about autism. I got to find out he was autistic and he went to school straight away…so I didn't know if he could learn, if he could write or anything. But he has done. We took Nathan and we went to have a look [at the Unit]. You get a feeling, don't you? We walked in, we went 'Yes!' We hadn't looked at any other schools. We were going to look at [local special needs school] but as soon as we seen that one, we realised that was it.

I just didn't know that he would express himself more, instead of going off to bang his head. I was just thinking, 'if he goes to school…' I'm too soft, me. I just give in – anything for an easy life! I thought, 'if he goes to school and learns respect for people and listens to them'… He wouldn't do anything like that for me. He wouldn't sit still. But when I walked in the class and saw the children sat in their seats waiting to go out and the teacher shouted their name I thought 'what's Nathan going to do here?' When they say 'Nathan' I seen him get up, go and get his wellies on and sit back down and waited 'til they shouted his name again to go out to play. I thought 'wow!'. It was just like, well, yes, you can do it. He's doing things here that he won't do that at home. As I say, I'm too soft with him, he'd have been all over… I thought well if he can do a simple thing like that, he knows what you are saying to him, he's understanding what you say, what will he do next! But as for like reading and writing, I didn't give it a second thought. If he doesn't, he doesn't, but if he does it's a bonus.

Oh reading was great! I read a lot of books to him. He liked me reading books and when he started he used to get my finger and hold my hand and point along like that. I can't remember when he first picked a book up and started to read. I didn't realise he could read so good. His writing's not so good. He can't be bothered with it. He knows exactly what he's doing but he can't be bothered. Too much hard work. It's easier on the computer, to type something and print it off, but his spelling has to be spot on. It really has to be spot on, his spelling, and if it isn't he asks me – looking at me and writing and turning to me. It has to be right.

Once Nathan started 'yes' and 'no' words that was a lot better. You ask him a question and say 'yes' or 'no' and he says 'yes' or 'no'. Since then, his speech has come on a lot better. He comes and asks you for things instead of just screaming and banging his head. I mean he asks me questions 'going to the shops, yes or no yes'. He asks the question to what he wants then you have to ask it back and he says 'yes'. It's just a conversation with him.

I just take one day as it comes. If he learns something, great. If he doesn't, he doesn't. What the school's learnt him, he's got enough now to build on what he's already learnt, to get on in life. As he gets older he's learning bits more and more."

As an example of how helpful the written timetable was for Nathan, Carol talked about a visit the class made to Nathan's house, as part of our class topic – Where I Live. Carol was particularly concerned that Nathan would find it difficult to accept that this was part of a school trip and that he would want to stay at home. In the event, everything went well, as she explains…

"He [Nathan] was first out [of the school bus] and he had a look about and he was just out in the garden. I mean, I didn't know what to expect. I thought 'He's not going to even get off the bus'.

But then I thought 'Well, if he did get off the bus and come in he'd go straight upstairs and just as he does when he comes in from school he'd take his clothes off and start watching videos'. But I was really amazed, because he didn't. He come in and had a look about and I thought 'Oh oh, his clothes are going to come off' but they didn't. He knew he was still with school and as I say he was looking at the timetable – 'I'm not staying here so I'm not going to take me clothes off' – sort of thing. 'I'm not going to get myself comfortable because I'm not staying' and yes, I was really pleased with him when he done that. And then, when it was time to go I thought 'Oh well, here we go! You know. He's not going to go.' And he was the first on the bus! He was just sat on the bus! I thought 'Oh!'

I think part of me wanted him to stay. I wanted him to think 'Oh he's home now. You lot can go home now. You've brought me home.' Part of me wanted him to do that, but he didn't and I was really pleased about that. I thought we'd have a bit of a do here, that you'd be trying to get him on the bus and he wouldn't want to. But he didn't and it went really well...

I expected him to do one thing and he done totally different to what I expected... 'Well,' I thought, 'if he can do that well he's not so set in his ways. You can turn him round to do different things if you explain properly, if you write it down.' He takes more notice of that. If you tell him exactly what you are going to do written down, he should accept it like he did then. But you've got to do it...yes... It's no good writing it down and saying 'this is what we are going to do Nathan' and then if he's not happy well we won't do it. It's no good doing that. If you write it down you've got to do it.

I was glad. I was glad he didn't create. I was glad he got on the bus and went happy. He always related better with a timetable, with a list of things. Because I remember we used it at the airport. The first time we went he hated it, so I wrote a timetable and it went loads smoother. It said 'two hours' wait' and it really helped him... It was very helpful. He knew what you were saying to him, but I think he just needed that extra little bit of security if you could call it. Written down, it meant more to him written down."

Chapter 4

The Water-baby

Lotti has curly blonde hair, clear white skin and blue eyes. She has no verbal communication skills and can only make her needs known by taking you to where she wants something and hoping you understand. She rocks and flaps her hands when excited and can laugh and cry when both happy and sad, making it sometimes difficult to interpret her moods correctly. She loves the elements but is difficult to engage in play. She is happiest in water or being tickled.

We are on a school trip. Lotti sees the water and her eyes light up. Not interested in the conventions of dress and undress she has one aim in mind – to get into the stream and enjoy! Now! Her impatience at having to be undressed is just about contained, but having to be redressed in a dazzling blue-starred swimsuit represents a totally unnecessary delay. It is a battle to keep her on dry land long enough to go through the social conventions of putting her into appropriate swimwear. She is perfectly happy to go 'au naturel' wherever she sees water. While this is fine at five, it will cause an almighty stir at fifteen. It is important she understands that water equals swimwear except, of course, at bath-time. Social convention is rife with contradiction and confusion when you are autistic! Her arms flail all over the place, her legs keep veering off towards the water's edge. We are holding her back for some incomprehensible rigmarole. Her face presses up to mine and away again, in a rhythmic bob, in time with the flapping of her hands.

Lest we forget that she is only going to tolerate this carry on with clothes for so long, between the laughter she throws in an occasional low growl. The implications of this rumbling are well understood by everyone who knows Lotti. If I don't get a move on and let her into that water very soon her patience, what little there is left of it, will have run out altogether and I will find myself, despite the continued rhythmic laugher in my face, on the receiving end of a very forceful pinch.

Lotti is happy, but not so sure of what my intentions are to totally relax her guard. After all she has been disappointed too many times before. There have been numerous occasions when she has begun to strip off and launch herself into water and we have stopped her. So her trust is guarded. Until she is in that water she will not relax.

All is well. Dressed and ready Lotti is released. She makes a bee-line for the stream, finds the spot where the water is flowing fastest and deepest between the stepping stones, and without a flinch lies herself down, face upstream, body stretched out like a contented seal and revels in the pleasure of icy cold water rushing past her tanned little body. Giggles of pleasure escape from her lips and we all breathe a sigh of relief. Lotti is enjoying herself. For Lotti is in her element.

Elemental is a great word to describe Lotti. She greets the extremes of our English weather like old friends, inviting them in to play with her. The wind streaming back her blonde curls, the rain beating down on her upturned laughing face, snow melting between her bare toes – these are all Lotti's welcome playmates.

It is a well-known given amongst primary school teachers that a windy playtime gives rise to hyperactive children who come back into the classroom wilder, louder, more fidgety and restless than on a calm sunny day. For Lotti, the wind has the opposite effect. It helps her to be more herself. Turning her face into the wind, giggling at the buffeting she receives, all the tensions of coping are literally blown away; the anxiety and agitation of constantly being at odds with our incomprehensible rule-filled social world evaporate. Her face unwinds and, despite the chill, we watch Lotti chilling out, freer to be herself in this undemanding elemental environment than anywhere else.

While Sam and Nathan get themselves into a tizzy when they are caught outside in a shower, Lotti fights to be released into a winter storm. Her personal thermostat is set at a very different level from ours. Her mum describes to us the night in December when she discovered Lotti had escaped from the house after bath-time.

> There she is, stark naked on the top of her climbing frame, laughing and flapping her hands for all she was worth as the snow fell all around her. She wasn't half mad when I brought her back in!

Water is also Lotti's soul mate. As summer approaches Lotti's game of choice is to wallow in her paddling pool with the sprinkler turned on, revelling in the sensation of water drops raining down on the skin.

So naturally her favourite school day is Friday. Friday is swimming day. After the first morning session we take the school bus to a local swimming pool and for a blissful half hour Lotti can revel in once again being in her element. Of course, once a week is pitiful if swimming is when you feel most at home with yourself. If only we had our own pool and Lotti could swim every day. But we are only a small LEA unit. So it is up to Lotti to do everything *she* can to make every day a Friday.

Lotti judges the days by what she brings to school. Friday is known to be Friday because that is the day she brings her swimming bag to school. At home, if she wants to go swimming, she brings her swimming bag to her mum and off they go. So it is perfectly logical for Lotti to reason that if she brings her swimming bag to school, we will go swimming. That is how she will make every day a Friday.

Lotti has extremely limited verbal communication skills. She relies heavily on 'objects of reference' to help her understand her life. Where other children in the class can understand either written or pictorial timetables Lotti struggles with these. So wherever possible we use objects to explain to her how her day is organised. For example, a soft play ball represents Soft Play sessions; a knife and fork represents dinner-time; a uni-cube represents number work; an armband represents swimming. That is our system, and on the whole it works. But for Lotti, her swimming bag represents swimming. If that is at school, swimming *will* happen. So everyday before leaving home, Lotti tries to bring her swimming bag to school. And understanding the difficulties she will face if she succeeds on any day but Friday – knowing that her anxiety levels will go sky high; she will work herself into a state of near demented agitation as the day progresses; she will be extremely distraught by the time she goes home – her mother and escort are faced with the unenviable task of ensuring she only comes to school with her swimming bag on a Friday.

'She's 'appy!' Lotti's bus escort exclaims every Friday as Lotti skips into the classroom on tiptoe and nonchalantly throws down her precious bag into the corner. You would never suspect the bag means so much to Lotti seeing the indifference with which she throws it into the classroom. But Lotti understands the morning routine and with her bag within sight she can relax, knowing that soon she will be off for a swim. And when the time comes Lotti is waiting by the classroom door, arms flapping excitedly, body rocking back and forth, swimming bag swinging about dangerously, straining to get going.

The pool is shallow along its length, with broad steps leading gently into the water, which gets deeper as you cross its width. We share this long pool with a local primary school, separated from them by a blue rope that is strung across the width. In their orderly half, obedient pupils divide themselves neatly into three groups – Beginners, Intermediate and Advanced – and are taught appropriately. Our half of the pool is a slightly more rag-tag affair. True, we have our own, albeit smaller, collection of Beginners – Nathan, who hates water and who is determined not to get so much as a toe wet; Intermediates – Liam, Toby, Lotti, Joss; and Advanced – Alice and Sam – not so much for their swimming prowess, more for their ability to follow instructions and make some systematic progress, as opposed to the more haphazard, idiosyncratic approach adopted by the Intermediates.

We are ably (and very gratefully) assisted by Warren, Liam's dad. The children adore him. He is the muscles of the operation, tossing children into the water with endless patience and enthusiasm while Sally, Erin and I try to put into practice each child's personal swimming programme. Despite appearances, we do have aims and objectives. The problem is the children don't seem to know this. They have their own aims and objectives and these are largely centred on the bright blue rope that divides our ramshackle half of the pool from the streamlined swimmers of the other school.

Whatever is claimed about children with autism lacking a 'theory of mind', all ours seem to instinctively understand that this barrier is there solely for their entertainment. The whole point of swimming, it appears, is to cross that barrier and disrupt as much of the other lesson as possible before a member of staff can cajole you back to your own side. Like children the world over, their one aim in life is to break the rules and foil the plans set by adults who think they have the upper hand.

Lotti is in the front line of this escape committee. As soon as she gets into the pool, guided by us to the end furthest away from the dividing rope (we aren't that stupid), her sole purpose in life becomes to get up to the rope, gain and maintain pole-position, and patrol the boundary, keeping half an eye on both sides of the blue divide whilst simultaneously trying to drown herself. She works her way up to the blue rope by throwing herself forward in the water until she finds her feet no longer touch the bottom. Then she suspends herself just under the water, arms and legs moving just enough to keep her afloat, not enough to propel herself anywhere useful, leaving us aghast with horror that she might sink – although she never does.

She does not often try to cross the rope but her presence there serves to alert the more mischievous (yes, you've guessed, Joss and Liam) to the fact that it is there, just crying out to be crossed. If we were able to leave Lotti to her own devices by the rope, thereby not drawing too much attention to it, we might be able to keep Liam and Joss distracted enough to resist the temptation to escape over or under the barrier. But Lotti cannot be left alone.

Lotti is utterly fearless in water. Which would be great if she could swim. But she can't. Lotti actively resists any attempts to learn to swim. If she is given a float she shoves it under the water, disappearing with it, and then shoots back up, letting go of the float as it catapults into the air. Straight away she disappears underwater again, holding her breath for what seems like hours, before repeating the burst for air. With a loud intake of breath she disappears again. She would repeat this over and over until hyperventilation caused her to drown. It is our job to ensure she doesn't. So, in spite of the fact that she loves water there is conflict. Her water-play verges not only on the obsessive but also on the dangerous. So, whilst swimming is a wonderful form of relaxation for Lotti, it is a stressful time for us, torn as we are between making sure she has fun and ensuring that our little charge doesn't drown.

We all suspect that if push came to shove, so to speak, she would be able to swim. After all, she can lie inert and horizontal with her head in the water, and float quite happily until, gaping, she is forced to draw breath. But it is not a theory we feel would be ethically acceptable to put to the test. We would all rest easier, however, if we knew the answer, since drowning seems to be some-thing she is determined to do. Oblivious to our concerns Lotti has the best of times in the water and is as relaxed and carefree as you could wish a child to be.

The pool session is over all too soon. A hooter announces it is time to leave. Having safely guarded Lotti from herself it is now time to safely guard self from Lotti. That Lotti loves her swimming session with a passion has, I hope, been firmly established. Lotti hates the hooter with an equal but opposite passion. The end of swimming is the end of Lotti's world. When the hooter goes, Lotti goes too. Into the deepest, most inaccessible part of the pool. There she violently resists all attempts to be cajoled back to the steps and out. We are without question the villains in the piece here, and Lotti does nothing to spare our feelings in letting us know that half an hour is a disgust-ingly short time to spend in a swimming pool and she has no intention of leaving quietly.

Despite our many attempts to make it easier for her, Lotti hates us taking her away from her beloved water. She nips, she bites, she screams, she pulls, she shoves and she kicks. In short, she does everything in her power to stay in that water. And there is nothing more powerful than a six-year-old child about to be deprived of her favourite activity.

Once she is out of her costume and back in her clothes she generally settles. It is as if the wearing of her clothes gives the final, definitive proof that swimming is indeed over. The anger subsides. And then the tears begin. It is one of those occasions when we are in no doubt that Lotti's tears are genuine tears of sadness. She wrings two little clenched fists across her dry eyes until she manages to squeeze out a tear.

'I cwie,' she wails, and our hearts go out to her. Sometimes we feel so cruel we wonder if the upset is worth the half hour of pleasure. But we know that to deny Lotti her swim would be even crueller, so we continue to try and find ways of easing the end of swim distress. We reason that, if she could articulate her feelings, she would probably be having no more than a good old whinge. Biting and nipping are only her ways of showing us her feelings. So we sym-pathise and accept the pay-off with good grace.

★ ★ ★

The weekly swim continues to be Lotti's favourite school activity. Horse riding comes a close second. This also takes place on a Friday afternoon. After dinner seven pairs of wellies are lined up, ready. Straight away, Lotti knows it is nearly time for horse riding. Then the riding hats are retrieved from the store cupboard, and the ritual of matching head to hat is completed. No doubt about it, we are going riding. Finally, we all troop out onto the bus that is parked outside the main door, ready to whisk us away for an afternoon of happy plodding around a straw-lined arena.

Occasionally (and for reasons I could never understand, it is only occasionally) the horses are allowed to trot. Lotti adores this, thrown up and down in wild abandon high up on the back of her solid little pony. Once, we went outside and down the lane. The fresh air and the thrill of seeing things from such a height clearly thrilled Lotti. She didn't want it to end.

These little tastes of a more exhilarating life on the back of the horse whet Lotti's appetite for more. If she could articulate her feelings, I am sure she would ask at every session to be able to go outside and trot. But of course she is only able to mutely do as she is told. No matter how hard she jumps in the saddle, or thrashes her legs against his side, the obedient patient pony does only what his leader tells him to do. Calmly, safely, uneventfully, he plods around the bare arena, steadily following the pony in front with a patience born of good training. Occasionally Lotti's impatience brims over and she gets agitated. The frustration of not being able to make the horse trot becomes too much. Lotti decides she has had enough. The session ends unhappily, a situation that could have been avoided if only she could have been allowed to take control and canter out of the stable doors and off into the sunset. On the whole, though, Fridays are wonderful. Swimming, horse riding and a contented Lotti. There is a problem though. (Isn't there always?)

Our school has one session of horse riding per week with Riding for the Disabled. This is generously funded by hard-raised cash from the Parents' Group. This means that each class has a turn riding once every third half term. Not every Friday. When horse riding and swimming are on together Lotti must feel she has died and gone to heaven. But when our turn for horse riding ends, things can get tricky. For when our turn ends a different class don their wellies on a Friday afternoon, collect their riding hats from the store cupboard and drive off in the very same bus we have returned in from our swim that morning.

Objects of reference are, as I have already pointed out, Lotti's means of understanding what is going to happen. Wellies, riding hats and the bus parked outside the main door all serve as pointers that mean 'Lotti is going riding'. All or one of these is enough to convince her that she will be riding. So when it is not our turn, we have to ensure Lotti does not see the wellies, the hats or the bus – or she gets very distressed.

Everyone in the school is aware of the difficulties we face, so great efforts are made to ensure that Lotti does not see what is going on when it is another class's turn. But of course, the best-laid plans… Inevitably in a small place so prone to high drama, there are occasions when Lotti is convinced she is going riding. When such occasions present themselves and the bus leaves without her we have to pick up the pieces.

This is where the Soft Play room comes into its own. Although small, this room is an indispensable asset. It is a safe, soft environment where the children can let off steam, give vent to pent up energies and diffuse tensions. It is here that we spend time on those non-horse-riding Friday afternoons. Lotti loves it. She loves to fall into the pool of plastic balls and roll around like a fish in the sea. She loves to leap from the highest padded cushion and launch herself into the ball pool. She is fearless and carefree, giving scant regard to anyone who might be stupid enough to get in her way. We have to be her eyes and be ready to save the equally unaware from possible collisions. In the ball pool Lotti just loves to be tickled. Relaxed and giggly she soon forgets about her disappointments. So, even without the horses, Friday is still the best day of the week for Lotti.

We try to make all our lessons fun, and cooking sessions are no exception. They are lively, challenging and often messy, but usually popular in different ways for different pupils. Icing buns is a favourite activity for all sorts of reasons, mainly to do with the opportunities it offers for trying to snatch an illicit lick at the icing. It is a great way of teaching all sorts of skills, from mixing, measuring and pouring to turn-taking, sharing and social interaction. For Lotti the *raison d'être* of icing cakes lies in the colouring. Lotti adores the bright colours of the icing, and the bright egg-yellow sends her into paroxysms of delight.

At the end of the session, when most of the children are eager to eat their erratically iced creations, Lotti collects as many yellow buns together as she can. She places them carefully in front of her, arranging them in a pattern that might look haphazard to the untrained observer, but which is clearly important to Lotti judging by the many meticulous minor adjustments that go into their final layout. Only when she is quite satisfied that they are all properly placed does she sit back. Arms flapping, she smiles and laughs with satisfaction and delight. Whatever the beauty these objects hold for her she is clearly captivated by them. She happily rocks and flaps, rocks and flaps as her eyes drink in the pleasure they give her. She guards them jealously, fending off anyone who dares try and snatch them from her. She does not eat them. They are treated with reverence, as if they are precious jewels to be studied and admired for their rare and exquisite beauty. It is both intriguing and humbling to watch this little girl gain so much mysterious pleasure from something as ordinary as a collection of badly iced yellow buns.

At the end of another busy school day we gather together at the round table and sing our goodbye song. This simple song proves to be a happy, easy way to gain a response from each member of class, in turn encouraging those with verbal language to use it in a rhythmic repetitive echoing back to the group 'goodbye', and those more verbally reticent to use actions to wave at their classmates. The song is a vehicle for practising a range of social skills, from basic eye contact and recognition of friends around the table, to responding appropriately to your name. It allows for actions to have equal weight with words, it is accessible to all and does not single out anyone as a failure or different.

> Lotti McFaddon, goodbye
>
> Say goodbye
>
> Goodbye
>
> Say goodbye
>
> Goodbye

And so on for each child.

At 'goodbye' each is encouraged to say 'goodbye', to give eye contact with others, to wave goodbye or to smile – whatever response is most natural and comfortable for the child. Everything about the song is made bold, explicit and fun, with staff giving exaggerated waves and eye contact to the named person and helpful waves in the direction of the named child.

Despite all this it is clear how very difficult it is for each child, at their own level, to overcome their particular difficulties. For Sam, our most verbally competent, giving eye contact is hard. For Lotti the challenge is to realise that we are all singing to her. When she does so her arms flap, she rocks in her chair and smiles. We help her to wave at the appropriate time. Over time she learns when to wave by herself – not to anyone in particular, but still it is a gesture of social exchange. On good days she waves and rocks happily. On bad days she might cry at the mere mention of her name and we are left with that helpless incomprehension that descends when unhappiness overwhelms for reasons we cannot fathom.

And then the day comes when, without warning and without precedent, Lotti says (not sings) 'Goodbye Alice'. She has never before, in any context, named a child in the class. She has barely indicated that she knows Alice from anyone else. But there it is. 'Goodbye Alice'.

So, what does Alice do in response? Does she say goodbye to Lotti? Does she wave at her? Does she turn to her in surprise? Well, no. She does none of these things because Alice is not at school. She is poorly. So we haven't sung goodbye to her.

Does this mean Lotti is merely filling in a gap in the song, following a routine, giving an automated response to a ritual that up to then has not been broken? It would be easy to accept that the communication is no more than that, except for one thing. Lotti is not repeating the lines of the song as we would sing if Alice had been sitting at the table. If she were merely repeating the ritual, then Lotti would have sung 'Alice Johnson, goodbye'.

But Lotti doesn't do this. She says, in a rushed, deep and surprisingly confident voice (surprising because it is barely used), 'Goodbye Alice'.

And then she says it again, and again.

It is always tempting to get very excited about such 'breakthroughs' in communication. If she can say this, what else can she say? Will she name everyone in the class? Should we be insisting that she makes more of an effort to say names? Will she start to talk more fluently now, in more situations? All kinds of hopes, possibilities and expectations can fall onto a little girl who has barely said a word for six years of her life and who has such an enigmatic diagnosis as autism. And of course everyone hopes that from this demonstration of understanding and recognition Lotti will be able to enter the 'normal' world of communication, with all the possibilities such a breakthrough will open up.

Lotti does start to talk more, and she does open up a tiny chink in her non-communicating armour. Over time, she is able to label more things and ask for some very basic needs: 'drink'; 'toilet'; 'shoeson' – one word meaning 'I want to go out in the car now, possibly to the supermarket, maybe to the fields to see the horses, perhaps to the beach – whatever it is you will only know by the rest by my body language and, if you get it wrong, by my pinches'.

She goes home and says 'Joss' to her mum on days when she has been working with Joss and the speech therapist.

But all these small but monumental verbal exchanges come later. For the moment we have 'Goodbye Alice' ringing in our ears long after the children have left. It is one of those moments that are very special because it is both unexpected and spontaneous. It reminds us that somehow, sometime, Lotti has stored away her classmate's name. Whether she was trying to say 'Oy, you haven't sung to Alice yet' or 'Hey! Alice isn't here' is something we speculate about after the class is empty. Really we are just stunned that Lotti has shown such an outspoken level of engagement in the class dynamics.

When Alice comes back we watch expectantly, hopefully, for signs of friendship, recognition or emotion. But Lotti shows no interest at all. She is too busy dancing in front of the mirror, flapping her hands and laughing to herself as she dances about on tiptoe.

Lotti appears to be admiring the strange attire we have put her into. Her blonde curls, tangled as always, catch the light. Her face is shining clean from its recent wash. She laughs and squirms as Sally patiently attaches the tinselled fairy wings to the back of her long white dress. Lotti happily concurs, making faces at herself as the final adjustments are made to her costume. For Lotti, unbeknown to her, is about to take part in the oldest school Christmas ritual. Along with countless other little girls up and down the nation's schools, in her long white frock, made in the finest tradition of old bed sheets, she is about to take centre stage at the annual school Nativity Play.

She is our Christmas angel. She has already pulled off the halo that was to sit on her head, irritated by its unfamiliar prickliness. This has been seized upon by Joss, our shepherd. He finds it far more interesting than the fluffy lamb we are hoping he will carry. Joss waves the tinsel about in front of the light, enraptured by its patterns. Minus halo and baby Jesus (who has already been rescued several times from the less than gentle ministrations of his guardian angel who is delighted to find such a solid missile to launch across the classroom) a rather manic laugh escapes from the cherubic lips of our Lotti. This is a bit worrying, as it can indicate a range of emotions from happiness through to anger. We all cross our fingers, hoping that Lotti will be able to sustain the illusion of angelic at least until her starring role is over.

The halo aside, she seems to be happy with the wings, and now lets us make a tolerable attempt at untangling some of the curls. She is dancing and smiling – at what we don't know. We do know it isn't at us, as she has not made eye contact with anything but the mirror. Although at first glance she looks like any little girl admiring her fancy dress clothes in the mirror, on closer inspection you can see that her eyes are not, in fact, focused on her dress, or her wings, or her white socked dancing feet, but on somewhere in the middle distance, at a point only she seems to see. The laughter could be about anything. More of concern to us, it is the kind of laughter that could go either way; either into greater mirth or be tipped over into frightened hysteria. Emotions are often muddled up in Lotti so that one minute she can be apparently happy, laughing with you, the next crying, or nipping, or in tears. We have come to understand never to take anything for granted with Lotti, not least when she is smiling.

Why we put the children through the Christmas ritual is beyond me. As we gather the class together ready to make the long trek to the school hall, where a waiting selection of parents, grandparents and knowing dinner-ladies sit expectantly, I think again of the awful typecasting that has informed our nativity tableau. Lotti is the angel, not by any virtues of personality but because she is the stereotypical angel – blonde curls falling around a face graced with cherub lips and innocent blue eyes. The fact that she can be a whirlwind of terror has not figured in our choice. Alice is the obvious choice to look after a baby Jesus as she is least likely to get an urge to throw it into the audience. So she is Mary. I just hope she remembers to keep hold of him. Alice doesn't really do dolls. Toby seems a good choice as her Joseph – after all he is the only one who obliges as Prince Charming so they will at least be happy to stand together. Joss's quiet demeanour suggests a boy who would tend his flock well. Sam and Nathan bring up the rear – Sam a solemn, conscientious king; Nathan, his crown disdainfully discarded a while ago, witheringly trails along like a tired old thespian who has seen greater days and is only doing this as a favour, don't you know? Nathan is, bless him, amusing us. Lotti, as we make our way to the hall, continues to look angelic. And at this moment it is the look that counts!

We give Lotti gentle quiet encouragement to play her part in this strange tradition. Once seated in the hall (praying fervently that whatever happens, please god, don't let the domino effect start now, today, with all these parents watching) Lotti snuggles up against my shoulder, laughing – ominously happily. I shift ever so slightly, just so that her teeth are no longer quite so close to my flesh, and smile at her. Sensing a mounting restlessness (in myself as much as in Lotti – when will it start and this ordeal of my first public scrutiny be over with?) I quietly sing Lotti's favourite song as we build up to the start of the first Christmas celebrations at my new school.

The angel is, as everyone assured me she would be, angelic. She stands behind Mary and Joseph dancing on her tip-toes, no doubt enjoying the pleasure of feeling her near-naked feet against the hard stage blocks, and smiles and sways as the music fades. She leaves the stage without a murmur of protest and we return to the classroom. We are all relieved that everything went well and all major disasters (too numerous to list, even after a mere term) have been avoided. Even baby Jesus survived the ignominy of being launched into the surprised arms of a doting parent.

Lotti's mum arrives with party dress and shiny new shoes (surely Lotti won't wear them! Her relationship with shoes is one of intolerant practicality. She will wear them outside if we insist but what is the point of them indoors?) Lotti's mum glows with maternal pride.

'This is why we do it,' I think.

For my part I too am glowing just as much, proud that my little pupil, no my little class were such – well, such angels.

Just as she looks the part as an angel so Lotti is transformed into the role of Ladybird Party Girl, from curly hair to pristine white frilly socks and shiny patent leather ankle shoes, via a full-skirted, velvet-bodiced party dress that would do any Snow White proud. Our own aspiring Snow White, in her plain skirt and blouse, looks on in wonder. Approaching Lotti (not an action Alice does lightly) and holding out the dress to full advantage she sighs deeply. 'She looks like a princess,' she exclaims dreamily. Alice has not a trace of envy in her voice. She is just happy to be looking at a princess, even if it is only Lotti dressed up. 'You shall go to the ball!'

Lotti is not at all impressed by 'the ball'. The Christmas Party is taking place in the school hall. It is decked out with balloons and tinsel and brightly coloured tables piled high with food and crackers. Lotti becomes anxious, uptight and very agitated. Balloons terrify her. She starts to tremble and pull away, desperate to escape from these things that frighten her intensely. No one knows why. There is no logical, understandable incident that can be traced back to give some kind of rationale to this fear, but Lotti and balloons do not go together. Despite their bright colours, Lotti wants nothing to do with them.

Judging by her body language, the hall has been transformed into a torture chamber, the balloons her torturers just waiting to set about their evil work. She cringes behind her mother, fitfully anxious. The offending objects are tactfully removed from Lotti's immediate vicinity and she is able to settle, albeit warily, to the business of 'Having Fun'. All too often it is a stressful challenge for children with autism to have fun. So Lotti ends another day, a day with its mixture of delight and terror, challenges and triumphs. As her mum settles her in the car to go home, she places a packet of Mr Kipling cakes on her daughter's lap. Lotti begins to relax. Her arms start to flap and her body rocks back and forth. Yellow cakes. What a delightful end to another strange and challenging day.

Lotti's mum talks about the deep and complex relationship she shares with her daughter as she accepts and celebrates her daughter's achievements

"When she does [something that is not repeated, like saying 'Goodbye Alice'] it gives me hope. At the back of my mind I think 'Well, it's in her and it's only up to Lotti when she decides to sort of let it pop out again'.

You know there's a level of understanding going in. She actually missed her in her way. She made a friendship. She actually missed the fact that Alice wasn't in the class. As far as I knew she knows the kids were there, but I didn't think she was bothered whether they were there or not. The fact that she missed Alice and knew she wasn't there – that was, in her way, like a bonding of friendship. It's what kids do. It was nice that, that she actually missed her... I mean she never says it for another six months but there was something there, and she missed her...

...You can't look at one child and make a general assumption – well she's in a world of her own because she's not talking, she doesn't give you eye contact, she doesn't take any notice, her eyes are everywhere, she's taking no notice of anyone. But how do they know? They should spend more time just looking. I think half of it is getting it back out of her. You can ask her a question but to get her to reply back! Well, I mean, whether it will actually happen who knows?

...She's quite vocal now but it's on her own terms...but she certainly expresses what she wants... We used to have a floor mat and it had a heart on and a star and she used to like this mat. And I used to sit there, take her finger 'star, duck, heart, moon', and I used to just go 'yes you can do it'... Because half the time she's not even looking where you're pointing, so you don't know, you don't know. It was just this one day that she actually said duck and 'Oh hallelujah!' you know? 'There is something going in.'

...She didn't really care that much. She paid more attention to the television than me, cartoons and that; I thought if I put a cardboard box over my head she might look at me. People – no! But objects like the telly, oh she gives them all her attention!... But as soon as she gave that little bit, as soon as she said 'duck' I thought 'well yes, you are, for all you might look as if you aren't taking notice you are taking notice'.

...You started using them objects in class...and that's how she was for a long, long time. She was, if [she] wants to go out in the car, she'd just pick the car keys up. To go swimming or something like that she finds her towel or her bag. She relied on that a lot until she was able to vocalise a bit more and she started reading more and more words. I mean, I could read a load of French – I'd read it badly but I wouldn't understand a word of it, but it's all right to read the words it's getting to know that she is understanding what it is she says...

Lotti won't form a relationship as such. All the kids are doing their own stuff but she'd play alongside them. I know she wouldn't necessarily play with them but she was quite comfortable going next to a few of the kids. I know for all she had a temper they were quite comfortable playing alongside Lotti. The fact that it was family, it was totally, totally relaxed. None of the kids were agitated or stressed over anything, it was as though learning was fun... I mean, can you remember – she's never done it again to this day – but she did a picture with all those twos? I brought it home. She was doing her painting and it was when she could hold her pen. She never used to hold it but she could grip it and she had a paint brush, I think it was a paint brush, and you just left. You were doing something and she was allowed to paint, she'd done her work and she had a paint brush. They weren't all the same way up – some of them were upside down, some of them were, there were a whole load of number 2s and a load of number 3s and she's never ever done it since, odd... [I feel] delighted. Over the moon! It's another confirmation that something is going in. I know for a fact now that it's only going to be on Lotti's terms but...

She mentioned Joss's name a few times. Well, I like to think she mentioned it because she was friendly with him but I don't know if they realised that ever. With them being so young. Did she know that she was a girl and Joss was a boy? Did her and Alice – I know that Alice was more able – but did Lotti twig that they were both little girls? I've often wondered about that. But she did like Joss.

I don't think she's actually lost the bond from that very first class... I do think because they were together in the same class for about three years they were, like, their own little family. That's how I feel but I do think she's bothered. I do think she likes being around the kids but doesn't necessarily want to interact with them... I do know she likes to watch other children play. I've seen her sit and watch for ages, flapping, watching her nephews play football... I do think she does form – well, maybe it's an admiration – I don't know, but I do think she forms bonds with some children more than others...

...She does like her own space but not all the time and there's other times when she won't go away, she just latches on top of you... At one time I thought I could be anybody. I could be from another planet. But now I don't. I'm her mum. I do think I'm special to her now.

I seen what she was capable of doing, where like at home you virtually do everything. Like she'd actually sit! She would sit and be part of the class. She was a proper little schoolgirl. You'd say 'We are going out to play now. Go and get your coat on.' And you'd take turns and you'd say their name – I always remember that – and they got their coat and their wellies or whatever. And for her to actually sit for 30 seconds until her name was called! Because at home, everything had to be totally instant – as in – she wants to go out, the shoes are there and you are out the flaming door! But for her to sit and wait for her name! You know what I mean, it was a really... I was over the moon!

Stupid things that I dare say people wouldn't even think about...you could see she was itching to get out. She was 'ohh' but she sat and waited for her name. And as I say, I thought 'Oh yes, you can do as you're told...you can conform to some sort of instruction if you want to.'... And then it was taking turns to mix the cooking. And all right, she didn't always want to have a turn or pass it on to the next one, but whatever, they all used to take turns. That was something she was never used to. 'If I want to stop here, or I've had enough I'm doing *this*!' But getting used to socialising, getting used to taking turns...so that was nice. All stuff like that, that she didn't do at home. It was like – oh yes, she's part of the class. She was included, like. You weren't exclud-ing her... She'd only exclude herself by not doing it. But she wasn't [taking a back seat], she was just a member of the class.

You see, when she was in nursery she wasn't a member of the class, she was just doing her own thing... For all she was doing her own thing [in your class] come story-time she sat. I was half expecting them all to be sat round the table and Lotti to be off...and she wasn't. She was doing the same... She was sat there with the others, a member of the class... They were all on an even keel and she wasn't the odd one out, where every placement she's been the odd one out. She fitted in. But to see her sat round the table like that, she would never sit round the table! ...It was like a normal class... Just everything they did, she was doing. She was part of it.

...You used to know who would wind which one and you used to make as much effort as possible to make it calm. I mean Lotti used to say '17' for ages and wind up Nathan, and Liam's pitch set Nathan off. But there's always going to be something you can't totally avoid, bar having a teacher in one class with this child having undivided attention. And then, is the child going to learn as well or are they going to get bored because they're wanting the stimulation of all the other kids around them? Because, like with Lotti watching the others – like Alice might have been doing numbers that day [she painted 2s and 3s] for all I know. You don't know what they learn from each other."

Chapter 5

Tigger – with Extra Bounce

Toby is the oldest in the class. He is six and has been at the school for a year. The first thing you notice about Toby is his big brown eyes that blink merrily. He is seldom still. Although he has communication skills he does not understand as much as he appears to. He talks fast and furious and is very single focused in conversations. He has boundless energy but finds it difficult to concentrate. He is sensitive to noise and can get quite emotional.

Toby opens the classroom door. The classroom is empty. Everyone is hiding behind chairs trying to stifle giggles. Balloons and banners hang in the air expectantly. We are all waiting to jump out and shout 'Surprise! Happy Birthday, Toby!' Then Father Christmas will enter the classroom with his sack full of presents just for Toby. Toby jumps up and down blinking excitedly and grinning with joy.

This is how Toby behaves when he comes in to school on a cold, wet Monday morning in the middle of term – as if it is his birthday and Christmas rolled into one and presented to him as one great big surprise party. Bounding through the door with all the exuberance of an Andrex puppy, his big brown eyes blinking at the innocent delight of it all, the words gush out of him, falling over themselves as they tumble from his Cheshire Cat grin. His greeting lands like an explosion of peas from a peashooter. 'What's your birthday now? Where do you live now?'

Behind the happy smile and the staccato words lies an urgency that demands an instant, accurate response. There is no time for the usual pleasantries: 'Hello, my name is Fran. What's yours?'

Toby wants answers and he wants them – yesterday. If you hesitate or insist, as some in the 'normal' world do, that it is more important for a little boy, whatever his difficulties, to learn to be polite and conversant with the proper protocols of first meetings, you might pass over this vital reaching out in friendship. Then you will miss the happy smile of recognition that Toby rewards you with for your readiness to conform to his particular take on good manners.

However, not to answer does not distract Toby from his inquiries. Persistently and with an ever-increasing tightness in his voice he will repeat the questions over and over. Not until the important facts of birth and address are settled will Toby be able to engage in further conversation. If you, in your arrogant wisdom, persist in going along the conventional line and ask Toby to give you his name first (as a surprising number of professionals, for example, do) Toby will simply behave as if you haven't spoken. He will repeat his inquiries in the same gushingly enthusiastic but increasingly edgy tone. He will continue, his questions becoming more truncated; his voice more and more staccato tight; his bounce turning to an agitated shuffle; his body language stiffening with frustration.

Persistent intervention can pull him out of this obsessive line of questioning. He can be persuaded to go along with your need for convention and give you his name. It is given in such a dismissive manner, however, that one would have to be completely insensitive not to realise that he is no more engaged with you than with a blank wall. Unfortunately many adults are insensitive. They relish in a superior kind of satisfaction at having 'made' this strange little boy conform to their rules. Toby will probably have nothing more to do with them (quite rightly). They, in turn, will have lost the chance to get to know this engaging little boy. For once you have imparted your vital statistics Toby settles into less manic mode and it becomes possible to have a conversation with him. You find yourself charmed and amused by him, as you would be by any little boy trying to make sense of a nonsensical world.

Toby loves to talk about trains. He makes occasional trips to London, to stay with relatives. The relatives never get a mention yet Toby tells us all about the train number, the stations it called at on the way and the time it returned home.

We know that London is an exciting place because of its network of underground railway lines that have maps made up of coloured straight lines and circles to mark the stations. Toby can recount all these facts to us in his usual fast and furious manner, his eyes blinking and twinkling with delight as he recalls his holiday journeys.

We are sure the London relatives are Toby's favourite relatives because visiting them is all about train journeys and timetables. In contrast to the enthusiasm he injects into telling us about the trains, Toby is quite unable (or disinterested) in recounting anything personal about his relatives, the family or any other activities that did not include trains. When we ask about his relatives his eyes glaze over, but once he engages in a conversation about trains his eyes light up. But if you ask him about the underground he couldn't be more animated! He recognises a fellow traveller and talks with all the lively enthusiasm of an obsessive. Watching him almost exploding with delight at the memory of the Intercity 125s lined up in King's Cross station it is possible to be a little envious of such devotion to a subject.

But it is a cripplingly narrow focus of interest. His parents describe the unhappiness and frantic bewilderment that Toby has to deal with in all those long, long minutes and hours and days that are *not* filled with the pleasures of trains, timetables and journeys along straight lines to it doesn't matter where. Despite his outward show of sociability Toby finds it extremely challenging to engage in the regular social world of family and friends. The bright, bubbly, bouncy six-year-old might charm and delight, but his narrow parameters of interest restrict his opportunities for happiness.

Despite these difficulties, Toby is overwhelmingly optimistic about life. Gregarious seems the wrong word to describe anyone with autism, the disability that conjures up a lonely, withdrawn child, but it is the one that comes to my mind every time I think of Toby. He hits the world running and if he can be enthusiastic he will be. He is a wonderful bouncy Tigger and like Tigger his enthusiasms carry even the most ponderous of us along in his trail of infectious good humour.

Toby never slinks quietly into a room. He erupts. His eyes dance brightly around the classroom, taking it all in. His body jiggles and jumps in an effort to contain its excitement at all the thrilling promise that another day at school might hold.

As soon as the children start arriving the day takes on a somewhat hectic pace. Dealing with important messages from escorts about change of home-time plans; urgent toilet trips for children who left home hours ago to arrive at school bursting for their first pee of the day and fighting the terror of letting go; guarding the door for possible escapees; being cheerful, sensitive and welcoming in different and very individual ways to each new arrival to the class; acting as strategic defence missiles, dashing here, there and everywhere to avoid problems as each new addition becomes a potential threat to the fragile stability of the classroom, the school day starts with a flourish.

Each child has a routine that helps him or her make the adjustment from home, to bus, to classroom. There is quite a time-gap between the first taxi and the last bus delivering everyone to school. Children arrive in dribs and drabs over a half-hour period. They come from all over the county and beyond, and arrive at any time from 8.45 (too early) to 9.15 (too late).

Because of the distances travelled and the unpredictable staggered start to the day, and given the practical and time consuming tasks that have to be attended to, a routine of 'free choice' activities has been established in the classroom. This is designed to meet each child's need for relaxation. In theory it means the mornings can begin in a calm and relaxed manner.

The children themselves determine the activities since cajoling anyone into anything they might find demanding, threatening or just plain dull is stressful for the children and therefore staff intensive, thus defeating the object. So in those first minutes in the classroom the emphasis is on low-key, stress-free activity (for the pupils at least).

Alice is easy. She has her crayons and pencils and a large supply of paper. Joss has his train set. Nathan studies a comic or his favoured book of the week. Liam gustily sings along to the music tape, causing minimum disruption once he has mastered the use of headphones. (Until then he has driven Nathan potty with his insistence on loud music first thing in the morning.) Lotti on a good day enjoys minutely rearranging and staring joyfully at a collection of bright objects, arms flapping in delight a happy smile lighting up her angelic face.

Toby, with his bull-in-a-china-shop approach to life, can tip this precarious peace into utter chaos by the simple fact of his exuberance. It is impossible to explain to Toby that Nathan hates being disturbed; that Joss gets over-anxious if he thinks his space is about to be invaded; that Lotti has a tolerance level equal to that of a scorpion about to be trodden on; and that Liam will only smile indulgently if you interrupt him between, not during, songs. We can no more stop Toby from being his effervescent, sparkling self than we can stop day turning to night. Once Toby hits the decks running the day well and truly begins.

After a quick précis at the door as to who is doing what, where he serves as a useful up-to-the-minute class register, we know we are ready to start the day. His fast, furious, accurate rundown of the present state of the classroom is very useful for us, preoccupied as we are with 101 minor problems that invariably come into the classroom along with the children each morning. (Hasn't the escort just handed over Joss to us? So why isn't he on Toby's list? Has he managed to slip past us, again, and make it unchallenged into the Soft Play room?) Resumé completed, Toby is ready to enter the finely balanced calm of the classroom.

Most days after Toby has been greeted by us and been 'encouraged' to hang up his coat on his own special coat peg – a difficult task when your eyes are flitting everywhere and your brain is processing 1001 pieces of information – he bounces up to each child to greet them individually. Already secure in their own particular niches, Toby enthusiastically makes his presence known to each in turn. Literally 'in their face' he greets each child accompanied by a fast and furious running commentary on what they are doing. Sometimes he is welcome. More often he is ignored. Invariably he upsets someone.

When his happiness and Alice's dreams coincide the morning begins with a quick waltz together around the classroom, Prince Charming and Princess Alice lost in a make-believe fantasy for maybe as long as 30 seconds. Then our bright-eyed little Tigger is off again on his rounds, making his larger than life self known to another member of the class. He informs the world that 'here is Nathan, he's looking at a book' and 'here is Liam, he is listening to Oranges and Lemons' and 'here is Joss, he is playing with the train set' and so on until, meeting with an agitated Lotti, he will bounce back to Nathan, grinning inanely, and Nathan will squeal in annoyance and go off to find another quiet corner to huddle in undisturbed.

The fact that, day after day, the only children who show any real pleasure in Toby's advances are Alice and the ever good-natured Sam never deters him. His up-beat personality refuses to be dampened either by Nathan's anger or Lotti's more physical rejection of his friendly overtures. This is when things begin to get tricky for an already overstretched staff.

Toby loves to be happy. He loves you to be happy. Should he make anyone in the class unhappy he chuckles and peers full into their face, exclaiming joyfully 'Nathan is crying'. Having his face peered at intimately by Toby is exactly what it takes to send Nathan into a paroxysm of tearful rage. Toby is not put off. He loves to say 'Hello Nathan' right up close every morning, as part of his daily round of the classroom.

It is one of the eternal mysteries of this disability that, in any given class of children with autism, there will be one child whose obsessive behaviour ideally and absolutely counter-matches another child's irrational fear.

In our class, this means that Toby's uncontrollable enthusiasm for planting his face within inches of your own face, before bursting forth with a delirious greeting, exactly matches Nathan's fear that anyone should notice him enough to want to put their face within a playing field of closeness to him, let alone add insult to injury by admitting they recognise him through the loud conjuring up of his personal and very private name, Nathan.

Nathan and demonstrative behaviour go together as comfortably as ice cream on a grill. Toby on the other hand is driven by a desire to acquaint himself intimately with your nostrils when talking to you. When we try to intervene we find ourselves with one more problem to deal with. As already suggested, it isn't that Toby just thinks this is the nicest, friendliest way to say hello to a familiar buddy. Rather it is that Toby is *driven* to say hello to his fellow classmate in this way. His life and personal happiness depend on this exchange taking place. Standing between Toby and his desire is like trying to stem a breached dam with a piece of soggy tissue paper. It just isn't effective.

To the uninitiated it may seem that the task is pretty straightforward. Take one child. Explain calmly and firmly that Nathan does not like to be greeted this way. Point out that a quick 'Hello Nathan' across the room will suffice. (In fact, it will more than suffice for Nathan, for truthfully Nathan would be happy if no one ever greeted him, used his name, or even acknowledged his existence.) But despite emphatic agreement 'Yes, Fran, yes, Fran' and even a cheery 'Hello Nathan' from across the room Toby, on release from the exchange, bounds over to his retreating friend with renewed vigour and…

Another tack is tried. Toby is escorted calmly to Nathan.

'Say hello, Toby.'

Toby says 'Hello Nathan' (face well back thanks to a restraining hand and well judged distance).

'That is nice, Toby, Nathan likes you saying hello like that.'

'Hello Nathan, hello Nathan.'

The greeting is repeated over and over as Toby is tactfully led away towards a table on which is laid out one of his favourite puzzles – Thomas the Tank Engine and Friends. (What did children with autism do before the Reverend Awdrey, I wonder?)

Together Toby and I concentrate on putting the puzzle together. I am doing my utmost to fully engage Toby in the task. Toby casts furtive glances in Nathan's direction. Suddenly, as I reach to pick up a jigsaw piece that has somehow fallen on the floor, Toby leaps up. His chair crashes backwards and in a dash that would put a gazelle to shame he is once again face to face greeting Nathan.

'Hello Nathan. Hello Nathan.'

Nathan's tears of anger and frustration alert Lotti, Joss, Liam, Sam and Alice to the knowledge that all is not well. In their own way each reacts to the disturbance. The fragile peace of the classroom is shattered.

The insurmountable dilemma faced by those of us supposedly in control of said peace and harmony is that the parameters in which we are able to deal with this two-edged conundrum are impossibly narrow. We are caught between a rock and a hard place. Either Nathan throws a wobbly because Toby says hello or Toby throws a wobbly because he can't get close up and personal to greet Nathan.

The end of the day is better. Toby goes home on the orange bus 'with Clive' and the timetable is a reassurance that this is fact. Toby is happy with this arrangement. He also appears to be happy when his dad makes occasional, spontaneous visits to school at the end of the day and takes Toby home in the car. He jumps up enthusiastically and bounces about, 'Go home with Daddy now.' I have been working hard to encourage parents to feel welcome in the classroom and in the school in general. I am proud of the fact that all the parents in my class belong to the newly formed Parents' Group where they can talk about their children and share in the highs and lows of family life. I am also delighted that many are actively involved in helping in the classroom or with activities such as school trips, swimming and horse riding. I have worked hard to develop open, honest relationships with everyone and actively encourage an open door policy. So to begin with there is no issue about the occasional spontaneous visit from Toby's dad.

Inevitably, though, things are not as straightforward as they appear. The day after Toby has gone home in the car his conversation revolves almost exclusively around the issue of 'Go home in the orange bus'. It becomes clear that the spontaneity of his dad's visits are making him anxious about what might happen at the end of the day. Because the days he goes home with dad are unplanned and spontaneous (they depend on when his dad is able to leave work) we are not able to devise a system that supports Toby in the way his timetable does. The 'bus' pic-symbol on his timetable has become untrustworthy as it no longer *always* means going home on the bus. Toby becomes increasingly agitated about not knowing what might happen to him at the end of the day. It begins to make him unable to focus on the rest of the school day.

The need to know what will happen next is a very deep-rooted one for all the children I have taught. Timetables are a very useful and effective way of providing this information, as children with autism are strong visual learners and can get reassurance from pictures and written words far more effectively than from the spoken word. They have proved invaluable communication tools and remove a lot of anxiety. But they have to always mean what they say to be trustworthy. There is no room for ambiguity in the mind of a child with autism.

I have a word with Toby's dad but Toby looks so happy to see his dad and go in the car, I get the impression his dad thinks I am just trying to shut him out or worse being plain awkward. This is the last thing I want to do. Perhaps I should just let things continue. But seeing the way Toby is unable to handle the unpredictability of his school day I know I must represent his best interests and continue the dialogue with his dad. We reach an understanding. If dad does come in for a spontaneous visit, Toby still goes home on the bus 'with Clive'. This settles the issue and Toby relaxes again. He regains his trust in the pic-symbols and his concentration on the rest of the school day returns, now that he is no longer preoccupied with how the school day might end.

This incident illustrates the importance of trust and good communications between staff and parents. Where this works well everyone benefits, but it can be difficult to work through issues particularly when you are both representing the child's best interests. However, the rewards of working with parents and having an open door policy cannot be overstated. As you will read later in the chapter, developing this relationship can be challenging for both parent and teacher.

One of the unforeseen pleasures of my work is to become, albeit for a brief time, part of the extended family. I benefit enormously from the help, support and knowledge that only parents can bring to the difficult job of teaching children with such profound and idiosyncratic difficulties as ours.

Perhaps now is a good time to describe how Toby reacts to life when it doesn't go *exactly* as he thinks it should. I stress the word 'exactly'. 'Nearly' and 'practically identical' have the same impact as 'not at all' in the world of the autistic mind. Just as Toby can hit the heights with his enthusiasm for life so he can plumb the depths. Watching him bounce around the classroom it is easy to imagine that here is a child whose innocent optimism means he is destined for a naively happy life untroubled by the ordinary set backs faced by children without his difficulties.

The notion of the 'happy innocent' is an attractive one, but I have yet to see evidence that any of our pupils, apparently oblivious to the outside world, are not troubled by the same insecurities and anguishes that we all experience in life, albeit in radically different degrees and expressed in uniquely different ways. Indeed, much of the emerging literature written by people with Asperger's Syndrome suggests that chronic self-consciousness is one of the difficult and debilitating aspects of their disability (Appendix 2).

Toby needs life to be happy. Anything less is too difficult to contemplate. And happiness means doing things exactly the way you want to do them. So when things go wrong for Toby huge tears collect in his big, brown eyes. When they start to run down his cheeks, which have become blotchy with distress, his nose starts to run in sympathy. Instead of a bright, broad grin his lips begin to tremble. A build-up of saliva begins to dribble, unchecked, down his chin. Reaching out for comfort towards the nearest adult, he presses his wet face into your clothing. A continuous stream of words of anguish pour from his lips to join the tears, snot and saliva that drip like an unstoppable tap onto his chosen comforter.

Through the tears and anguished sobs Toby makes sure you know what it is that will stop the deluge. If it becomes apparent to Toby that he is failing to achieve his goal then, despite the loud uncontrollable sobs and their accompanying sticky deluge, Toby begins to negotiate.

Under normal circumstances Toby is quite unable to engage in a rational discussion about actions and consequences – although if you took the nodding and compliant verbal agreement at face value you would conclude that he is the most adaptable, amenable child you could ever hope to meet. At the height of his uncontrollable slobbering misery, however, he becomes the Arthur Daley of emotional wheeling and dealing. He is not only prepared to compromise. He appears to understand just how that compromise can be bought. He seems to know that a slobbering, crying, distressed child is the last thing you, the adult, want to be responsible for.

If we are a bit slow in coming up with alternatives that might satisfy, then Toby (between gut-wrenching sobs) makes sure we know his terms. With the odd word here, the mumbled suggestion there, he manages to keep bargaining until eventually we come up with some kind of satisfactory deal. He appears to understand the value of playing heavily with the fact that when it comes down to it adults (and especially teachers) cannot bear to see a child unhappy. So we capitulate to his demands.

While he adjusts his demeanour back to the happy-go-lucky child we begin the mopping up process. As we do so we are aware that, somehow, we have just been manipulated into agreeing to give or do something that we had absolutely no intention of capitulating to when the whole watery drama begun only minutes earlier. We have to admire his technique. After all, who would want to prolong an encounter with such a mix of bodily fluids just on a matter of principle?

Such is the strength of character of this little boy, constantly battling with such a devastating disability, that Toby is able to overcome many of his difficulties and make progress educationally and socially. He is hampered by a particular over-sensitivity not uncommon in autism. Toby has a problem with noise.

Many children with autism have difficulty processing and tuning into, or out of, certain sounds. Often these are sounds that are unnoticeable and certainly wouldn't trouble the rest of us. Particular sounds can drive Toby up the wall and distract him so completely that he is unable to focus on anything else. This over-reaction to sound is not only distracting, it also appears to be physically painful. Its effect on Toby cannot be ignored.

When his tolerance to noise is low he clamps his hands over his ears and tries to create his own noise – a stream-of-consciousness outpouring that would impress our greatest free thinkers. This appears to give him a cocoon of comfort against the noises and a way of managing whatever discomfort he is experiencing. When he is in this state, however, it is almost impossible to engage with him. If you try to prise his fingers away from his ears, it is like trying to pull the world's most powerful magnet away from the pull of the North Pole. If you try to distract Toby with something tempting to cheer him up, like a sweet, for example, as quick as a flash his hand grabs the sweet and returns immediately to clamp itself back against his ear. If it weren't born of such difficulty, watching Toby wrestle with a sweet paper whilst trying to keep his ears firmly protected by his hands would be a marvel any contortionist would be proud to emulate.

It is second nature for us to consider such problems in the day-to-day classroom organisation and planning. Each child has an education plan that takes into account these problems and addresses them in appropriate ways. When it becomes apparent that a radiator hum is the cause of Toby's distress, distracting him from being able to concentrate, we rearrange the furniture so that Toby has a working area well away from the radiator and in the centre of the class.

Even so, keeping such a live wire sitting at his place, focused on a task, can be quite a challenge. But there are things Toby needs to learn to develop to his full potential. Reading, writing and number work are amongst the important areas of the curriculum that Toby tackles with the same level of enthusiasm that any six-year-old could reasonably be expected to. That is to say, he is either carried along by his own enthusiasm or he has to be cajoled into enthusiasm by his teachers. There are things Toby enjoys learning and things he is less keen on. In the quiet, supportive environment of our classroom he is able to apply himself and make steady progress.

With gentle persistent encouragement and a clearly organised working environment away from irritating noises and irresistible temptations Toby's progress is steady. He learns to read, he can do simple arithmetic and he can absorb facts. He enjoys participating in sports. He laughs at stories (for which I am especially thankful) and he makes bold and original statements about matters that interest him, such as what time the train to London leaves when he goes to visit his relatives. His gregarious nature and conversational skills lead him to be the first pupil in the unit to try integration with a mainstream school.

When I become his teacher, Toby is in his second year of integration at the local mainstream primary school. He goes for a morning session once a week, accompanied by Erin. His gregarious personality means he manages well at playtimes and in the energetic PE lessons, where his lively enthusiasm and eagerness to be with other children enable him to join in alongside the rest of the class with some success. However, as the class ages and the time spent in more structured learning increases, Toby's difficulties become more apparent. He is not able to concentrate at all in the classroom. Although he appears to have good language skills he is unable to make sense of the stream of instructions and explanations that precede any individual tasks. Erin becomes a necessary constant support for Toby, repeating and 'translating' what the teacher says. She also has to encourage Toby to rein in his exuberance so that other members of the class are not disrupted. The work becomes harder and harder, the pressure to conform as a member of a large class more and more difficult. The gap between his social, emotional and educational development widens further as the year progresses and Toby begins to flounder.

On the surface, his bounce and bright blinking eyes and fast talking chatter present a capable persona. But he is simply not equipped with the numerous skills needed to function successfully in such a busy environment. Problems associated with an overload of input and difficulties with social exchange mean that Toby has to concentrate ever harder in order to rein in his natural instincts to be lively, bouncy and chatty. He relies increasingly heavily on Erin's patient intervention to help him manage the situation.

Back at school, trying to eat his dinner in the busy bustling dining hall (not the most ideal environment if you need to unwind), it becomes apparent that Toby is becoming increasingly stressed out by his time away from his familiar surroundings. This stress manifests itself in Toby's increasingly unreasonable and unsatisfactory attempts to pull together his familiar world around him, like a cocoon.

He tries to alternately shut out and reorganise the world of the dining hall, desperate to make it the safe familiar place that will calm his jangled nerves. He calls out frantic 'Hellos' to anyone and everyone he recognises. He leaps off his chair to grab familiar people for a hug that gives him no comfort. His eyes flit about and his agitated body cannot keep still. He is unable to concentrate on his food. His sensitivity to noises peaks so that he can barely use a knife and fork, his hands are clamped so tight against his ears.

In his attempts to restore order nothing satisfies, everything is wrong: the food he has chosen to eat; the arrangement of it on his plate. He can't decide who it is he wants to sit with or where he wants to sit. His eyes are everywhere and nowhere, he is talking to everyone and listening to no one. He is distracted by the hustle and bustle of bodies moving randomly around him. He is trying to block out the noise. Finally the overload of stimuli reaches crisis point. Toby can no longer hold it all together. In anguished agitation he becomes a fearful trembling child, trapped like a caged animal with nowhere to go, no means of escape.

Then it begins. His frantic attempts to regain his sense of self. He becomes tearful and tight-throated. 'Say hello to Toby, say hello to Toby.' He pleads at anyone for recognition as if, in the act of being greeted by name, he might somehow regain that part of himself he has lost. Toby desperately needs to re-establish his sense of self. But it is not enough that children and adults acknowledge his quick-fired greeting with a friendly hello. Neither is it comforting when he hugs tightly to the nearest trustworthy adult, holding on like a limpet. A barrage of requests pour out of him, the urgency of his unknown need leaving us all feeling desperate in our collective inability to make things right.

Even with the support of an assistant to guide, explain and help control the idiosyncrasies of Toby's behaviour, the pressures of trying to deal with all the social and emotional demands of relating to so many other people in a busy classroom have become too much for Toby. Once the relative structure of the PE lesson gives way to the more usual hustle and bustle of an ordinary primary school classroom Toby's primary difficulties come to the fore. Toby has to draw on all his coping strategies and the stress this is generating for him is beginning to outweigh the benefits. The children he is mixing with are also dealing with more changes and challenges than they have in Reception. The gulf between Toby's educational, social and emotional skills and those of his peers is growing ever wider. It is a difficult decision to make, as so many hopes are invested in the possibilities of successful integration, but in the end it is agreed that the benefits of integration are outweighed by the stress it is causing Toby.

Toby returns to his small class of friends. In this supportive environment Toby is able to be himself. He continues his education in a setting that gives him as many advantages as possible to allow him to develop his personality and enjoy, as every child should, his educational experiences. Within the structure and order of our small classroom Toby is able to give expression to his true self – a happy, bouncy boy with bundles of uniquely directed enthusiasm.

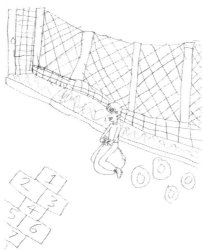

Toby's parents talk about the importance of good parent–teacher communication. Together we look back at the time when Toby was getting upset about home time

Fiona: What you sort of said 'do you mind when you come in not taking him home' 'cos that's what it [the problem] was. A few times we'd come in and taken him home and he'd built up a relationship with the escort, so when that was broken, I mean he does it now even 'Go home', 'Do this', 'Do that' and then he starts stressing. I think he's more able to express himself these days probably. When you had him he probably wasn't able to voice his…

Greg: I remember this happening. I think one of the issues, I think what was happening at the time was the school was still quite small. It was a very sort of, you knew everyone by their first names, it was quite a relaxing casual atmosphere and I was already going in. I used to help a lot with the riding so it was that sort of relationship and I didn't realise at the time that I was causing yourself and Erin and everyone else problems by coming in and I thought – not that I was doing you a favour but – I thought I'll come in a little bit early and take him home and there were a number of times I did that. And when you mentioned it initially I was sort of taken aback. I just felt, well I found it a bit odd. I thought we were part of the school and we were being supportive and it wasn't until I sort of sat back and thought it's exactly right. The whole point was being Toby's routine was being disturbed, which was destroying everyone else's routine at the end of the day, which was probably just as important as the routine at the start of the day. I certainly felt a little bit nose pushed out of joint.

Fiona: Did you?

Fran: I was very conscious of that. I was very – not that you made it obvious, just because of the way I am. I'm sort of very sensitive to how things are and I was very keen to have parents coming in and help and to be welcoming and you had come in and you worked [in the classroom]. Everything was fine but I felt we were having a bit of a communication block. I was seeing things from one way and you were seeing things from another and I could see your point of view and understand that and part of me was thinking 'Am I doing the right thing here?' but I felt I was representing Toby in a way when you didn't see him and the effect of [you occasionally taking him home] and there was a bit of 'Oh why am I not getting this across right' because I know you care for your son and I know you wouldn't want him to be distressed.

Greg: The way I was seeing it was Toby was quite happy, you know 'Hey I'm going in the car with my mum and dad' you know. I suppose I never really thought of anyone else.

Fran: No it wasn't even that. It was just the next day when he was going home on the bus getting stressed – was his dad coming in? – and we didn't always know. You would sometimes come spontaneously, which was what I wanted. I wanted you to be able to do that but the knock on effect for Toby at the end of the day was becoming 'oh is this a day I go home/not go home' and he'd start to build up anxieties in the day.

[Toby interrupts the interview]

Fran: There are two issues when your child starts school. One is the teacher has a different view of your child and you have to get used to someone else saying 'Oh I know a bit about your child as well' when you know so much and it's been such a deep and intimate relationship and a traumatic one in lots of respects, and we are like the first people to, if you like, take a different view of your child and I think that can feel quite threatening for parents – I don't mean that in a patronising way at all because I've been there with my own children – but it's just you are handing over your baby and building up trust is something that does take time. You can't expect it to just instantly happen, so there does have to be a settling in period. I think it's important that there is one and that both teacher and parent are aware they have to work through that.

Greg: I suppose you were acutely aware of the sort of problems it was causing, whereas personally I was just picking Toby up and he liked the idea of it you know, and I liked the idea of going at the end of the class and helping out with the reading and stuff like that. But I can imagine looking back it caused havoc.

Fran: No, but it caused a few problems.

Greg: Yes.

Fran: It was a problem for Toby. If it had been a problem for the rest of the class it wouldn't have been an issue, because we would work around that. It was the fact that Toby was getting unsettled at the end of the school day and we didn't seem to be able to help him through that.

Greg: It was such a close-knit school and we knew all the teachers by their first name we felt comfortable, I suppose that was it. The teachers at secondary school and primary schools would have a professional detachment whereas at special schools it was such a small school.

Fiona: Yes, we noticed the difference when [our daughter] went to school. You tried to be supportive and go in and help and blah blah blah. But it wasn't the same.

Fran: How important was it for you that you could be open to the teachers and they would listen to you?

Greg: I think probably the background I came from certainly, sort of teachers were professionals...you had a respect through fear of your teachers. They knew everything.

Fiona: Yes, it's like now in schools people daren't go in and say to the teachers...

Greg: Yes and certainly, as I've been a Governor and Chair of Governors, I've come across some fantastic teachers – some fantastic people – some really special people. But I've also seen, like, people who aren't very good. You are teaching my child and you see now I've got a respect for teachers who work...

Fiona: It's like anywhere, like any walk of life...

Greg: You sort of – I don't know if it's the sort of background I come from, I think it is – that anyone in your position with your qualification...

Fiona: I suppose you see them as authority figures as well, don't you?

Fran: Well, we've all been pupils, haven't we?

Fiona: Yes. Exactly.

Greg: The idea of knowing the teacher's first name, well it's a shock isn't it? I mean at school it was always Mr Daykon or something like that and that was sort of usual. But at Toby's school the head teacher was always known as Esther. It was really nice and I look at it now and I go into school and I talk to the children and there's 50–60 staff and I probably know about 20 of the staff these days, properly, you know properly and it's totally different. In the early years especially you knew every child by its first name and every teacher by their last name.

Fran: Do you think that affected your level of confidence in the people who were looking after your child?

Greg: Oh most definitely. We just, we felt assured that they were doing a good job. We had really good contact with the home–school book...

Fiona: I think as well though you knew they were caring. You knew like they cared about them. You know what I mean?

Fran: One of the reasons I think people are nervous about having parents in is because they know parents are watching and it is intimidating. However good you think you are it's still very different to have somebody there who you know. I can remember thinking, when I started, thinking gosh everybody – all these mums and dads – they all know so much more than me and I feel such a fraud that I am making decisions on their behalf. I was really grateful to have the input of parents because you get to understand a lot more about the individual child, autism in general and then it becomes a two-way thing and I think it's very rewarding and everybody benefits. But it's not easy. Because you are dealing with personalities and you can't expect to get on with everybody just like that.

Greg: The other side of the coin is when you're a parent in that position and you are helping out I think parents, sort of, think 'Are we doing the right thing here by supporting this thing here?' It's maybe a fear from your side but also from our side to make sure that we are doing a decent job.

Fran: Sure. I think that's what people need to know. It is a sort of two-way thing and it's not just that the parents are there to keeping an eye on you or you there to keep them at bay because they might see something, see that you're not all that brilliant.

Fiona: I think they do a great job.

Fran: But I think it is an issue. Personally I think it should have more focus than it does – parental involvement – certainly in a school like ours. I think it's very important that those barriers are broken down, so I want to strongly advocate that. I think that most parents, even parents who like you who have come from a background where the teacher is like this – where they're not used to coming into school and are not comfortable to find ways of opening up the school so that it is comfortable – I think it's very important because it is a partnership, it isn't just one way.

Greg: Parents need to take responsibility. Like there's a line you shouldn't really go over like, professionally. You should understand you are a lay person and if you do, say, you come out of the classroom and you go to [the head teacher] and say 'I didn't like the way Fran did this certain thing here', I feel that some parents would be quite willing to do that. They would sort of without really knowing what it is like professionally to be a teacher. I can think of a few parents who would maybe help in the classroom and have no problem at all going to [the head teacher] and saying, 'I didn't like the way that was done.' I think there's got to be a place for parents but I think parents have got to realise that they're not the experts, teachers are. I'm not saying teachers are fully the experts but you are trained to do a job and parents do another job, you know.

Fran: Yes. I think recognising that we are coming from different places is a good thing isn't it? I mean like you saying about Toby doing things at school he wouldn't necessarily do at home. There are opportunities opening up for him there but maybe aren't at home but the flip side of that is there is lots going on at home that you can't provide at school, like the fluidity of life. So do you think there should maybe be something more formal for parents and teachers, maybe some short training or something before you come in the classroom or a general code of conduct or as a way to get it more…

Greg: I think a semi code of conduct. Over the last couple of years as a governor I've been involved in classroom observations and we've a set of rules sort of how we should deal with situations. Last year I did a presentation to the staff to explain we are not coming in to spy, we're coming in to try to do our job basically, to see if the teaching is good. So I certainly think there should be a code of conduct for parents in the classroom. I'm sure there is, but what you don't want it to be formal or it feels you have to sort of sign before going in.

Fiona: Everything is a balance though…

Chapter 6

The Diplomat

Sam has a sunny smile and a shy demeanour. He is stocky with a shock of blond hair. Diagnosed at three, he started school when he was five. Sam's communication skills are developing well. When he concentrates he can listen and follow conversations, but when excited or anxious he slips into cartoon jargon echolalia and it is difficult to break into his fast and furious flow. He is peace-loving and easily upset by conflict and criticism.

Sam is off to the loo again. He has been there three times now in less than ten minutes. Back at his table where he is working at independent tasks – today he is working his way through some addition problems – I call over to him.

'Everything all right, Sam?'

'Yes, I'm all right thank you Fran.' This is said quickly, head well down, no eye contact, face colouring with embarrassment.

'Would you like some help?'

'No, it's all right thank you Fran.' Sam is always polite. He understands the rules about being polite to adults and he sticks by them rigidly.

'Are you sure?'

'Yes I'm sure thank you Fran.'

I turn back to Lotti who is having a one-to-one session with me and who does not take too kindly to interruptions, however well intentioned. Less polite than Sam, she is liable to give me a meaningful pinch if I fail to give her my full attention – either that or just get up and walk away.

Sam gets up to go to the toilet again. Oh dear. He is stuck on a question, and he can't bring himself to ask for help. Instead he sits churning away at the problem all by himself, hoping he can work out the answer without having to admit to anyone he does not understand. Anxious as always to do the right thing, always wanting to be perfect, hating the idea of admitting he might be struggling to anyone, the anxiety levels build up.

Sam is one of the more able pupils. Even so he has difficulty communicating, particularly at times of high anxiety. Being a perfectionist Sam always has to get everything right. He can't accept that it is okay not to know something. He is more tolerant than, for example, Nathan about learning new skills, but even so he can't bring himself to ask for help if he gets stuck. He will do all he can to work things out for himself. If that fails then he begins to worry. Careful not to draw attention to himself, he chews at the problem, getting himself more and more worked up until the tight little knot of fear of failure sends him off to the toilet.

At that point, Sam's natural tendency towards conformity is overridden. He does not ask if he can, please, go to the toilet, with his usual polite adherence to correct classroom etiquette. He slinks off shamefaced, utterly mortified at his self-induced sense of failure.

No matter how often we tell Sam it is okay not to know something; no matter how upbeat and light-hearted we are at helping him; no matter how much positive feedback we give him on the rare occasion when, head bent with embarrassment, he will mumble shamefully 'I don't know how to do this'. No matter what we do it is always a torture for Sam to come across something he cannot tackle without help.

It is surprisingly difficult to teach someone with autism that asking for help is something we all need to do. Sam has good verbal skills. He is able to answer questions about events and people that are significant in his life. He is even able to tell us about the difficulties his fellow pupils are having. He is always kind and thoughtful. He can on occasions initiate conversation – a very unusual skill for someone whose primary difficulty is social interaction. But he cannot understand that asking for help is *a good thing*.

Sam is able to learn new skills and knowledge on a one to one basis, where they can be demonstrated to him in a non-challenging way. He is also able to learn in a group, having less problems with focus than most of his classmates, where half the battle is making the lesson more interesting to them than a radiator hum or a piece of thread on a cardigan. As long as the new knowledge is amply demonstrated and methodically explained then Sam is fine. He can then absorb and use that knowledge independently at a later stage.

Facts are great. Sam loves facts. They are given, absorbed and never change. If two plus two equals four today, then it will equal four tomorrow, the next day and the next year. No problem. And if you teach Sam how to do addition sums by one method, for example, using unifix blocks, then again, no problem. But if you set Sam a puzzle, such as 'There are two girls and two boys and they each have a sweet. How many sweets do they have altogether?', then it is definitely toilet time.

Generalisation is a key area of difficulty for anyone with autism. This becomes very evident when Sam begins to make such good progress that he is able to work independently at some tasks. He is given carefully chosen work that requires him to practise skills that he has grasped in one-to-one sessions first. Hence the independent work on addition. As he becomes more confident about working alone, and as his knowledge base broadens, he begins to use published maths textbooks. When it is his turn to work by himself we write down what pages he has to work from and he settles down to the task with enthusiasm.

It is a big step for anyone to work independently in this way. It means he has to maintain focus on the task without constant prompting. He has to have his equipment sorted – pencil, exercise book at the correct page, textbook open at the correct page, eraser to hand to correct mistakes (although this is rarely used by Sam, as he only writes down what he is sure is correct). Having sorted all these things he then has to resist the temptation to go into his own little world and instead must try to concentrate on the work before him.

Sam's workspace is a small alcove that is free from distraction. There are screens to block his view from the activities of other members of the class. These are designed to support his chances of being successful. They minimise external distractions and maximise his chances of being able to stay focused on the tasks in front of him. To ensure Sam does not get anxious about what he has to do when he finishes his work there are written instructions that lead him to his next activity – whether that is Soft Play time, free choice or snack time. These activities are designed to be rewarding, something to look forward to. They act as self-motivating incentives to finish the task. The clear structure is reassuring and necessary to prevent Sam worrying that we might spring some horrible surprise on him – a horrible surprise being anything unexpected, however pleasant and enjoyable. Within this structure, Sam begins the huge challenge of working independently. It is a big step forward in his development and everything is in place to ensure he succeeds.

It is only when he starts working independently in this way that the full impact of his difficulties relating to the autism come into sharp focus. Once it becomes clear that Sam is having particular problems admitting he needs help, this becomes one of his learning targets. These targets are as important, probably more so, than the academic targets he has. They represent clear strategies for tackling some of his core difficulties in social and emotional development. Tackling these issues helps Sam develop into a more socially competent and independent member of the class. They also make it more likely that he will be able to manage any integration into the wider community. After all, how crippling will life be if we never learn how to ask others to help us?

Teaching a person with autism means giving equal value to teaching social skills – the sort we all take for granted. Problems often arise out of difficulties a person with autism has in relating to others. Sometimes these result from a literal interpretation of a general rule that is understood to function only as a way to maintain general order. So, for example, in a busy classroom a teacher may ask pupils to work on their own and not ask for help, when it is commonly understood by everyone that some pupils will ask one another for help, some will not get on with the work at all unless the teacher reminds them, some will get stuck and ask for help and some will wait until the teacher gets round to their table, realising that she is keeping an eye on everybody and is there if needed. Without the ability to generalise, children with autism are left to fend for themselves, alone and often worried that they are doing things wrong.

Even in the small, supportive environment of our little classroom Sam feels the internal pressures to conform and do well. These are greater than any sense that we are kind-hearted people who are there to make his learning as comfortable and successful an experience as possible. Once it is evident that Sam needs to learn to ask for help, we set about helping him see this as a positive part of the learning process.

It is an enormously difficult task. We have to convince Sam that it is okay to say, 'I can't do this', or, 'I don't understand', or even – surely a neutral enough question – 'Can you help me please?' But we have to help him overcome a huge resistance to the idea that this does not mean he is a failure. Being something of a perfectionist and worrier myself I have a huge amount of sympathy for Sam's dilemma. How can you ask for help when it is the last thing you want to do? How do you convince yourself that *it doesn't matter* when it is the thing that matters most?

Gradually, over time, Sam does learn to ask for help when he gets stuck when he is working independently at his table. He does this within this context because he learns that that is what he can do. He does not transfer this knowledge to other situations. It is also clear that he is not really convinced that it is a good thing to do. Whatever we say, asking for help really cuts into all those areas of his autism that he finds so difficult – acute shyness; perfectionist nature; inability to think laterally; conformity; initiating social interaction; self-awareness; self-confidence; verbal dexterity; coping with unpredictable situations; confidence in other human beings; awareness of roles of others – the list appears endless.

So we have to continuously reassure Sam that we can help and that it is a pleasant experience, not a threatening one. We look out for him showing signs of needing help and make it as easy as possible for him to take the initiative. There is always an uneasy awareness of how readily Sam can allow himself to just sit and worry over a small problem until his stomach ties itself into that little knot of fear that will send him once again scurrying to the safety of the toilet. It is a testament to his determination to learn that he does not allow this difficulty to overwhelm him, and he continues to make steady progress at working independently despite this difficulty.

On a social level Sam enjoys taking part in the shared session with some children from Forestpark, a nearby school for children with moderate learning difficulties. Along with Alice he gains a lot from the social contact with a group of more articulate children of his own age and slightly older. He is soon able to move from the sessions within his own school to visiting their school. With our support and the expertise of the Forestpark class teacher he spends some time in a classroom that is bigger, busier and more challenging than his own. A well-structured Design Technology lesson gives him the opportunity to meet the challenges of sharing his progress with a number of children. Gradually he gains confidence to talk more with his classmates – stilted and rather one-sided conversations that are the beginnings of tentative friendships.

It is very upsetting that such positive and supportive progress in socialising within a supportive wider community has to come to an end, but as explained earlier decisions made with budgets and targets as the main focus leads to a reorganisation in the LEA. As Sam's parents discuss later, the knock-on effect for Sam is that he loses his recently acquired social contacts. The progress that he has begun to make outside his little classroom is curtailed. Given his personality, Sam would have benefited in so many ways from this form of integration. Less demanding than a large mainstream class, more challenging socially than his small class at the Unit, Sam would have undoubtedly continued to benefit from this experience. It is very difficult for LEAs to make provision that fits exactly with the needs of all children, but I feel this is a form of integration that should be looked at more carefully, having benefits for two pupil populations without overburdening the children with pressures that become too great for them to manage in a fully integrated system.

Back in our school Sam negotiates the hurly burly of classroom life. Not wanting to be drawn into conflict Sam deals with potential arguments over toys, books or missing a turn by stating philosophically, 'It doesn't matter.'

Avoiding conflict is important for Sam and he would much rather give up something he really likes than be the cause of someone else's distress. He goes out of his way to avoid conflict. His natural preference is for harmony and joy to fill his life.

When happy or excited, Sam beams from ear to ear, flaps his arms and bursts into a fast and furious stream of jargon. Although it is largely incomprehensible, this tumbling torrent of words comes from cartoons and TV programmes. They are often verbatim re-runs of catch phrases or scenes from programmes that Sam has seen again and again. It is impossible to break into this stream of words. It is like an avalanche of thoughts spoken aloud. There is no expectation that anyone might want to respond to him, to join with his train of thought. These words tumble out whenever Sam is happy or excited and all we can do is to stand back and let them wash over us.

If you ask Sam a question and he does not know the answer, or he is too shy to respond directly, then he might well respond with a jumble of this incomprehensible jargon. It is as if it is a cover for Sam's self-consciousness or a protection from potential intrusion into his personal space.

It is possible to engage Sam in conversation, though, once he feels comfortable with you. Although he is shy, once he gets to know you he can be quite chatty in his stilted, autistic kind of way. If you ask him about his home life, he will always want you to include Chloe: 'She's my sister, you know.' If you mention his mum then he will also offer you information about his dad, lest dad, in his absence, might feel left out.

Sam is blessed with a kind and gentle temperament. He likes the classroom to be a happy and peaceful place. He does everything he can to ensure it stays that way. He will give up toys, books, his seat, even the shirt off his back if he thinks it will help everyone stay calm and relaxed. It is hard to believe that anyone can be so naturally sweet and good. He is never aggressive whatever the provocation. He walks away from conflict rather than be dragged into it. If he can find a diplomatic solution, he will.

Lots of things please Sam – especially other people's happiness. If everyone in the class is happy then so is Sam. At snack time, when it is his turn to hand round the biscuits he insists on being scrupulously fair. This can be a problem, as his idea of fairness is that everyone should have a biscuit regardless of whether they want one or not. It takes him a while to accept that it is not a personal insult if someone says no, or pushes his willing hand away in disgust. Sam wants everything to be just right. So even learning about the difference between being fair and individual choice is a challenge. Sam never really seems to accept that it is quite right that some children have a biscuit and some don't, but he learns the social rules and obeys them even if they make no sense to him.

When Nathan rejects Toby's enthusiastic greeting it is Sam who will be there, saying an amiable hello as often as Toby requires it. If Liam gets agitated trying to find his favourite tape, Sam will help to look for it and beam with pleasure as Liam's indifferent hand snatches it from him and he silently slinks away without so much as a thank you. When Lotti starts to gnash her teeth and prowl restlessly Sam will be the first to inform us, 'I think Lotti's not very happy Fran.'

And when one of us hurtles out of the classroom in hot pursuit of an escaping Joss, Sam will laugh and flap and chatter delightedly, knowing that it is all a game that will end happily with the safe return of Joss and the exasperated smiles of the adult. This contradiction of awareness of moods and difficulty with interpreting social rules throws up just how complex and contradictory rules of social interaction can be. When we come face to face with Sam's difficulties we wonder how it is that any of us make sense to the complex, unspoken rules that determine so much of our social exchanges. Trying to decode them for someone else puts into sharp relief the enormity of the difficulties facing even the most articulate child with autism when they are functioning with a very different set of codes that we can often only guess at.

Sam is hugely reliable and dependable, especially when the dreaded domino effect threatens. Many a time he has helped us avert chaos by intervening in just the right way to keep the next potential volcano from erupting. When everyone else is happy it means Sam can be happy. Then he can settle down to pursue his own little world in peace and harmony. If he had a theme tune it would surely be the famous Morecambe and Wise signature tune 'Bring Me Sunshine'.

Everyone who knows Sam knows that he comes with his own little ray of sunshine. Everyone wants it to always be that way for him. But unfortunately real life is tougher than that. Whether he likes it or not Sam is living in a world full of conflicts, uncertainties and hassles that have to be dealt with. And dealing with these things is not what Sam does best.

Sam is here because he has autism, which means for Sam, as for all the children in the class, that it is difficult to function without clear guidelines. As already demonstrated, he can get very anxious. He has to know exactly what is expected of him. He also needs to know what is happening throughout his day. If he does not know what is coming next, he will be unable to enjoy his present activity for fear of the potential difficulties of the next one. He therefore relies heavily on his written timetable.

Sam is hyperlexic, he can read anything. His eyes are magnetically drawn to any text, from the class register, to letters home to parents, to labels on biscuit packets. In a fast and furious mumble he reads through lists, instructions, directories, signs, anything. He does not understand what he reads but that does not bother him. He is compulsive and unstoppable.

Our challenge is to help him move from developing his hyperlexic skills to learning to read for meaning. This is why we have given him a written timetable. It proves to be a great motivating factor in helping him to understand that all these words he reads so quickly and correctly are there for a purpose, to carry meaning, to convey ideas and facts.

Every morning the first thing Sam does, apart from the polite ritual of saying hello – a ritual he slavishly adheres to because he has been told it is good manners and it is what you should do (but which, truthfully, we all know he can quite happily do without, thank you very much) – is to check his timetable. He then gives a running commentary to whoever happens to be near by (or to no one) about what he thinks of the various items on his timetable. Being so well behaved, or rather such a slavish adherent to rules, Sam does not exhibit the less inhibited forms of protest some of his less socially aware classmates can and frequently do resort to. Sam would not dream of throwing a wobbly just because he doesn't like writing, or reading, or number work, or PE or cooking or whatever tortures we have dreamed up in our attempts to provide a broad, balanced and relevant education for our pupils. He watches horrified, for example, if someone tries to tear the pages of an exercise book, or throw a jigsaw across the room to register their non-compliance with the task at hand. Sam, poor good Sam, is a conformist through and through. A well-developed and rigid set of rules, gleaned from teachers, parents and listening in to what makes people get cross with you, have left their mark on Sam. If there is a rule, *he* certainly is not going to be the one to break it.

His mum has told him he has to do what the teachers say. This is great for us. It means that at worst we have to listen to Sam stating the obvious 'It's too boring' and at best we can worry about one less pupil settling down to work, as we know that if it is on his timetable Sam will do it. However, it is this personality trait exaggerated by his autism that makes Sam so vulnerable to over-anxiety.

Happily Sam is enthusiastic about most things that we do at school. He is the one we use as a yardstick when trying out new activities or approaches. If he is bored then the rest will be climbing the wall! But in one lesson Sam is at odds with most of the others. Whereas Lotti, Toby, Liam, Nathan and Joss have an endless supply of energy and are always enthusiastic about physical activity, Sam prefers a more sedate life.

He does not like PE. He especially does not like PE when there is any element of competition about it. Sam hates losing. It is the one thing that makes him cry. And sulk. He just cannot hide his disappointment. Not that we go out of our way to have winners and losers. PE is designed around individual achievements. Where there is an element of competition it is usually designed to encourage self-motivation, something very few of the children seem to have.

For example, an activity might be to throw balls into a bucket trying to improve on your personal best. But no matter how we word it, no matter how secretly we might record other children's scores, no matter how encouraging we might be, no matter even if there is no one to compare with, Sam knows everyone's ability, everyone's score, everyone's personal best. If he can't beat them it is an utter disaster for him. He is hugely disappointed with himself. Even when he is only trying to improve against himself, Sam is mortified if his next attempt isn't always better than his previous go. He throws himself about, declaring 'I can't do this'.

Tears well up. He stomps about in despair. He has to try again until he does better. We try to teach him to accept that he does not always have to be the best. We encourage him to celebrate the success of others. We give him rules to help him cope with disappointment and he learns the phrase 'Maybe next time'.

Gradually, reluctantly he learns to control his disappointment with himself. The tears lessen. He learns, without conviction, that it is the taking part, the trying your best, which matters. He will clap and cheer the success of others, trying so hard to be magnanimous. He is only able to do this, I suspect, because he thinks it is a rule about PE. The conformist in him struggles with the perfectionist! In his heart of hearts he always wants to be the winner, to do his best, to be the best.

It might come as a surprise, given his need to conform, to discover that Sam can be argumentative. It is some time before we see this side of his character, despite assurances from his parents that he has a very stubborn streak in him. Like Joss and his running, it is not until Sam feels relaxed within the classroom environment that we see this side of his nature, and then only rarely.

It is his only real vice, and it comes with such charm that we can never take it too seriously. If asked to do something he doesn't want to he tells us very politely, 'No thank you. I'm just too busy at the moment.'

When you persist so does he.

'I said I can't Fran, I'm very busy.'

He stubbornly digs his heels in, and uses all his verbal skills to persuade you that he cannot possibly do what you are asking. Especially when you suggest going for a walk. Sam hates walking. As ever, though, he understands that he is too young to have the last say; he knows that, ultimately, grown-ups have to be obeyed. By way of continued revolt he starts to whinge.

Sam's mum had warned us about his ability to whinge but we hadn't really believed her. All we see is this sunny natured, eager to please little boy who is clearly going to win the Nobel Prize for Peace when he is old enough to qualify. It isn't until the class is well established and we begin to venture further afield than the local park — a mere tiptoe away from the school bus — that we come across the problem of Sam and his whinge.

Not one to mince words (none of the children who can talk are bothered about social niceties, and all couch their complaints in brutal language that leaves no room for misinterpretation) he moans about walking anywhere.

'This is boring.'

'Walking is boring.'

'I'm bored.'

'Is it far?'

'I'm too tired.'

'My legs hurt.'

Every parent knows how irritating this drip, drip of childish moaning can be. Irritating though it is, these expressions of dissatisfaction from Sam are never accompanied by the degree of non-verbal protest that others in the class deploy.

When Nathan doesn't see the point of walking any further he will let you know in no uncertain terms. He will drop to the floor, squeal loudly and twirl himself about like a demented snake so that it is impossible to do anything with him (except bribe and cajole and bribe some more).

Sam's whinging complaints are persistent and wearying but no more than that. He does, however, have a very effective, non-violent, means of protest. He walks at a snail's pace, getting slower and slower the more disgruntled he is. He drags his feet, scuffs his shoes, and has even been known to develop a very convincing limp! And nothing can persuade him to go any faster. Once he is in that mood, then he is in that mood. It is the only streak of rebellion we ever detect in Sam, and so we can hardly complain. Obviously as his whinging

with us is rare and restricted we are not unduly stressed by it, but we have it on good authority (his mum) that he can be really stubborn and go on and on when he feels like it.

Apart from when we are out walking, we do not see this aspect of his character much in school. While it would be nice to think that it is due to our firm but fair approach to Sam, I think it is only honest to admit that it undoubtedly goes back to that character trait described earlier in Sam. He has such a well-developed sense of people's place in life. We are teachers and his mother will have told him that teachers are to be obeyed. Despite the fact that he is the only one in the class who holds this view, the best efforts of the six rebels he spends every day with do nothing to dissuade him that this is the way things must be.

For once autism makes our job easy! Sam's sense of right and wrong is very well developed and who are we to dissuade him? I think we also benefit from the 'stranger' element, in that no matter how relaxed Sam is with us we are still 'teachers' and in his mind still deserve a level of respect that his mum never gets, by virtue of her familiarity and safeness. However well we get on with Sam (and as you will appreciate, Sam is very easy to get on with) we still induce a feeling of shyness in him that I don't think he will ever be able to overcome.

Sam's good-natured enthusiasm always helps us through the more difficult days. Having someone with an upbeat, sunny disposition around you is something to be cherished, and Sam is so easily likeable that none of the other children, however out of sorts, deliberately try to upset him. Certainly he does not become a regular target in the way Nathan does for Toby, for example.

I think all the children sense and benefit from his diplomatic approach to classroom life, and know that he will never go out of his way to cause them distress. This makes it all the more poignant to watch Sam trying to cope when someone does turn on him and upset him. He is startled. He looks both surprised and dejected. At the same time he is hugely, crushingly embarrassed that he has become the focus of a drama.

He has tremendous difficulty coping with his emotional responses. Desperately trying to repress the effects of both the physical and emotional hurt caused by any attack on him, he tries to cover up the incident as much as he can. If he becomes aware of our concern he does his best to pretend nothing has happened. If he is offered explanations of comfort, 'He doesn't mean to hurt you Sam', it only serves to make him more cringingly embarrassed that he is involved in 'an issue'. Through desperately suppressed sobs a little voice will choke back, 'I know Fran, it doesn't matter.' And a brave little Sam will try and busy himself in the nearest distraction to hand, to cover up the mortification of not only being targeted for hurt, but also of being *seen* to be targeted for hurt.

It is almost as if dealing with our distress (caused by the inevitable guilt at not having intervened in time to avert the incident) is as great a trial for Sam as dealing with his own emotional hurt. The weight of his suppressed, barely concealed feelings is almost unbearable. To then look on and see Sam approach the cause of his unhappiness with some kind of a peace offering makes us all feel too humble for words. Why, we wonder, can't the world be governed by little Sams exuding peace and goodwill to all?

It would have been easy to allow Sam to be walked all over by the more robust and aggressively self-centred in the class, but we realise that to be that vulnerable to the demands and moods of others is not wholly a good thing. Learning to stand up for yourself, at least in some settings, is as important as learning to compromise. While Sam would have been happy to let us allow Lotti, for example, whisk away a book he has chosen to read, and to go along with his magnanimous 'It's all right, I'll get another one', we have to help Sam learn to stand up for himself. Intervening causes distress to both parties, but apart from the fact that others need to learn about sharing and turn taking, Sam needs to know that he can, if he needs to, stand up for himself and alter the course of events in his own favour.

This balancing act of social exchange and social adjustment is not easy to teach, especially when the mounting crossness of one leads to the adamant insistence by the other that 'I'm all right. It doesn't matter.'

Explaining to Sam that he does not have to say 'I don't mind' to everything seemed utterly pointless when he retorts back 'I don't mind' every time, but we would have been very insensitive if we had failed to pick up the fact that on some occasions Sam does mind, that he does indeed feel helpless in the face of another person's unintentional bullying.

On those rare occasions when, with encouragement, Sam does stand his ground, he often goes away from the encounter with whatever object the potential dispute has been about only to find himself so racked with guilt that he is unable to enjoy it at the level he has been doing before the unfortunate 'incident' occurred. It is difficult to see this extreme sensitivity played out so tortuously in such a kind-hearted, loving little boy, and this inevitably leads to a protectiveness towards him that probably does him few favours in the long run.

On the whole though Sam's kind and sunny disposition helps him and those around him to lead a peaceable existence. His contribution to the happy atmosphere of the classroom is always appreciated. To see him flapping his hands and laughing in delight at the sight of Nathan giving a quick, furtive 'hello' to Toby – so obviously delighted to see both his friends happy – Sam's generosity towards others can't fail to spur us on to ensure that we continually strive to create a happy classroom environment where continued learning can flourish.

Sam's parents talk about the dilemmas of finding the best education for Sam

Alan: [May] was looking round the schools, and I didn't really want him to go [to the Unit]... I didn't want him to go there at first, because with it being autistic I thought he was going to go into it more and copy, you know. That was what I thought. I wasn't sure. I just didn't want him to be with children with even more severe autism, in case he would copy.

May: The thing was, at other schools we looked at I thought he would have got ignored, you know. Because he would have blended into the background. Because all the children were more forceful than him. Because our Sam was quiet then and I thought he would sink into the background. My worry was that he would get ignored...so I wanted him to go to the Unit and I ended up sitting in the offices at Education telling them I wouldn't move until they sent him to the Unit cos they were pushing me to agree to somewhere else...they were more or less saying to us well he's only mildly autistic, where in my mind I thought he was best where they specialise... It was just a relief, really, once they actually said yes he could go. But then we were frightened they were going to put him out of the Unit...because they kept saying he was doing really well. We kept thinking, well he can't be doing too well or he'll be out!

Alan: Yes, we were quite worried once he got there. He'd been there, and he was doing a bit of integration. I was worried in case they thought he was doing so well that they would make it more long term, or he'd be moved to a more high functioning school, you know. And I knew he couldn't cope. And we didn't know at the time that the teachers knew he couldn't really anyway. He seemed to be doing a little bit better than all the others.

May: ...We were worried that they might be steering us towards something else, but they weren't. We were coming home thinking, I hope they aren't thinking to send him somewhere else. We've fought to get him in there and they might be wanting to send him somewhere else, that was what was going on in our minds until we realised they weren't. At that time there were only 21 kids at the Unit and places were tight so we were thinking, oh cripes they might be thinking – well, if Sam can go somewhere else they can put someone else in his place.

Alan: You could see he needed to be there, after a short while. He would never have managed in another school, even with one-to-one help. It wouldn't have been nice for him, you know. Kids would have turned on him. He'd have got upset very quickly. He just couldn't have coped. He couldn't have coped... Two of the children were on the same level as him. I expected it to be a place where they were all banging their heads against the wall or biting you, and all that. 'Cos you heard about this. I was frightened he'd see these kids and copy. I could see it wasn't the case. There were children on a par with him, if not some better. He just seemed happy there, so we were happy he was there. I was worried he might start banging his head against the wall or fighting other children, you know. But he didn't and he came on. He learnt things. He really come on. He didn't speak very much when he went. His eye contact was bad. His writing was non-existent, you know, but he started to improve...

May: Really, overall, you've always been more optimistic. I'm the pessimist in the family. I think the worse and then I think, well I can't be disappointed. He says I only look on the black side, but I think, well, nothing worse will happen if I look on the black side. It's just like, if he [Sam] was just ticking along, then I'd be happy. But he hasn't. He's improved and in fact he's kept that steady improvement, which sometimes some of the children seem to plateau out. But I keep expecting that, but you don't, do you? You keep thinking he will keep on. But I think he'll plateau out.

Alan: No, he has made steady progress. He has, continually, you know. But it still shows through. It shows through. He's 20 to 30 yards ahead of

us, babbling along to himself. You think you can have a conversation
with him, but it's all...

Sam had the opportunity to integrate with a nearby school for children with moderate learning difficulties for an afternoon a week

Alan: It was never something long term we wanted for him. How could I
        put it? It was not that we wanted him to leave school and go out and
        do it all the time, but that he could mix with normal children, to have
        normal friendships. Which he wasn't at the Unit. There were very few
        at the same level to have a friendship with him. So that's why we
        wanted it, I suppose. He didn't have many friends. He hasn't got no
        friends at all, because he can't play out. We tried letting him play out
        and even now they're at him. There isn't the time for him to create a
        friendship, for them to allow it. He doesn't get it so...

May: Yes, he used to talk about the people. He'd meet someone in the street
        and you'd be thinking 'who's that?' and it would be, 'oh he's from
        Forestpark'.

Alan: 'That's my friend.' He used to call them 'my friend' so, you know...
        He had no friends. There were a couple of children in Sam's school he
        can have a little bit of talk with, but not anything much. But some of
        the others from Forestpark would properly talk to Sam more and Sam
        could answer them back. You know, 'How are you doing?' 'Oh, I'm
        doing fine!' Yes, it was definitely good that way. And he said they
        were his friends.

        I think it only became an issue after a while, wasn't it? At the
        beginning, it was good to see him settled. And then, you know, with
        his school being so far – friendships can't form after school. There is
        the school environment – and then it's finished.

Fran: Would your ideal be a local school with a class attached?

Alan: Yes, definitely.

May: Then he could have got the best of both worlds. He could maybe
        have mixed in the playground and met children who lived local...
        Originally, when we moved up here, a few of the parents didn't even
        realise that we had a son. Because obviously he didn't play out. They
        didn't see him go to school. And a few of them actually said to me,
        'Oh, we didn't realise you had a son.' So it sort of proves he's really
        isolated, because he can't play out on the front, so he's not meeting

other children. And I'm not meeting the parents. Some of the children around here have been all right with him, but you have the odd one who's not.

Alan: He got upset quite quickly. You're talking about maybe a matter of three to four weeks... You couldn't expect to have what the school gives – the specialising in autism – which is good for him as well as [being local]. It's not possible. But, no question, if it [a specialist school] could be close by it would have been better for him. It would be nice if it could be local, but there's no way. There aren't enough children.

May: We know children where they've [had support in a mainstream school] and then they start dropping [the support] in a couple of years, like leaving the dinner times and the play times off. Which, to me, they start getting picked on in the playground, you know. If they've got an assistant with them in the classroom, but then when they're out in the playground on their own, left on their own, then to me, that's more the time when they are needed. But then I think it makes them stick out even more, like a sore thumb, because they've got this person trailing them.

Alan: They're too vulnerable, aren't they? They're too vulnerable. I wouldn't have liked it.

May: I wouldn't have liked it. I definitely wouldn't. I know people who have done it and they say they like it, but every time they tell you they are getting bullied. I tell you, I wouldn't like it. My *major, major* thing would be him getting picked on. And it's still the major thing. Wherever he goes, he'll get picked on. Even now, they know. He walks two miles in front of you, doesn't he? It's no good. He talks to people and even if they answer his questions they are puzzled by him, when he's down in the town centre and he's flapping. You know, it's just the fact that he's waving his hands about.

Alan: Overall, the Unit has been the best thing for him. But it would have been nice if there could have been some long term integration. It just seemed to stop. If he could still be with those friends that he had made – not start again and have to make new friends...

Finally, Alan shares an anecdote that gives us another glimpse at Sam the Diplomat, this time within the family life

Alan: He still wants life to be nice, Fran. In fact he's so clever: me and her [May] were arguing and I lost my temper and shouted and Sam said something in the back of the car. I was still mad and I shouted at Sam to tell him to shut up and stop being cheeky. You could have cut the atmosphere with a knife. And we'd almost got home and Sam says to me 'He's a big-head, dad, isn't he?' and I said 'Who?' in a sharp voice and he says 'Humpty Dumpty!' and we all laughed and it broke the ice. And he engineered it. He knew that there was an atmosphere and he broke the ice. He loves it to be nice and easy…

Chapter 7

The Wind-up Merchant

Liam was diagnosed by an educational psychologist as 'classically autistic' when he was three years and six months old. He could not start school until halfway through the summer term when he was five years and six months, having missed the September intake due to administration errors. He was the last of the class of seven to start. Liam has a cheeky grin, deep blue eyes, a round, white, freckled face and ginger hair. He is generally a happy, energetic little boy with a sense of mischief and a gung-ho approach to life. He flaps his hands when excited and hums a deep monotonous hum. Liam has a limited vocabulary, but can make most of his needs known through single-word requests. He has a few phrases, like 'No, Liam' and 'Be good', and he echoes back adult questions and phrases without understanding.

Liam comes with a warning. Not exactly a health warning, although it could be seen as such. It is more the kind of 'don't say we didn't warn you' warning. The sort of unhelpful warning that suggests it is really quite irrelevant whether you have this information or not because it won't make any difference. 'The die is cast' is the sub-text of the message we receive from Liam's pre-school nursery. This doom laden but somewhat flippant acceptance that we are 'in for a shock' is further reinforced by the cryptic cheerfulness of his adoring parents. 'Ha! You don't know what he's like but we do!'

But we have spent six months at the job. We have been on training. We have A Plan. We don't quite know how we are going to execute this plan, but at least we have one. It is better than the plans we dreamt up in the early days of Joss's classroom breakouts. This is a pro-active plan. This will not address the problem as and when it arises. This plan will, if properly executed, prevent the problem from ever occurring. It will do more than just nip it in the bud. It will kill it dead. And if it doesn't work we will, apparently, be forever rescuing our ginger-haired, blue-eyed, round-faced innocent from table tops, work tops, window ledges and even radiator tops. For Liam, it appears, is 'a climber'.

Now, to some, this might not seem such a bad thing. Lots of little boys are adventurous and like to set challenges to stretch their prowess at balancing along walls, curb edges, garden climbing frames, trees. It is a natural and healthy part of growing up, developing the body and the mind. If Liam climbed in the style of other little boys we would encourage him. But of course, he doesn't. He climbs because there are places to climb. He climbs to avoid doing things. He climbs to wind you up. And Liam climbs because he finds the attempts of adults to catch him and coax him onto the floor, utterly, satisfyingly, hilarious. In fact, more than climbing, Liam loves to wind people up. We soon learn that if he can do anything to frustrate you, he will. So, for example, if you want him to sit still, he will jump up. If you want him to put his shoes back on, he will take his socks off as well. If you want him to pick up a pencil, he will knock over a jigsaw. If you want him to be quiet, he will shout. If you want him to sing, he will button up his lips, tight. Which is a great shame.

Liam is a lovely singer. Caught unawares, you can be treated to a tuneful rendition of the latest jaunty pop song, the sort that lodges in your brain all day and comes back to haunt you when you are finally settling to sleep after a long day at work. Although his diction is questionable, his voice is as sweet as an angel's, and from the look of rapture on his face you could believe he is singing with the gods themselves. But never when you want him to. Never at the right time, or in the right place. Which is a pity, because the concentration involved in singing puts a stop to his pursuit of winding up as many people as he can in as short a space of time as possible. But I digress. Liam comes with the warning. We are determined that he will not see our classroom as a training circuit.

We have had considerable success implementing aspects of the TEACCH philosophy in our classroom and we have seen the benefit of a tightly struc-tured approach. We have learned a lot from the TEACCH course (see

Appendix 3), presented by Dr Gary Mesibov (Mesibov, Schopler and Shea 2004). He has explained that it is possible to use a child's autism to help develop desirable behaviours. One of the many challenging aspects of autism is that children set up routines – often bizarre, sometimes unsociable and sometimes just plain awkward routines – that once established are hard to break. Dr Mesibov suggests that this can, on occasion, be turned on its head, so that routines that are desirable to the adult can be encouraged.

Association is another key feature in autistic behaviour. If Liam enters our classroom on day one and climbs, it is very likely that he will incorporate this behaviour into his daily routine associated with entering the classroom. This behaviour is then very difficult to stop, as the climbing comes to represent more to the child than the action alone. It is as if, by removing the activity, you are removing something of the child's understanding of who he is in this par- ticular setting. So, it is far better to pre-empt the problem by ensuring that behaviour is the sort that is acceptable and manageable.

Now, this may sound easy and straightforward. But many children with autism have a very limited repertoire of acceptable behaviours. Many are anti-social, destructive or self-limiting. Before Liam comes to us we have little idea of how we might channel his behaviour into something more acceptable. We do know, however, that we are determined that he will not see climbing as part of his school behaviour. For that first week, every moment of Liam's day is shadowed by one of us. We do everything we can to observe, entice and cajole Liam into getting interested in any one of the exciting classroom activi- ties that don't involve climbing. But he isn't interested enough in books, train sets, jigsaws, Duplo, colouring or sand play – which is a bit of a relief, truth- fully, since sand play can be quite tricky when the interest in sand becomes how it tastes or how fast you can empty the sand-tray contents over the classroom floor!

The only thing that holds Liam's attention is singing. He will stop, turn to whoever is singing and even at times join in. But we can't have a member of staff on hand just to sing to Liam in those unstructured moments between lesson times. We have a tape recorder, but of course while Liam would be happy as a sand boy to listen to music all day, Nathan, Lotti and Toby would be far from happy to start their day with someone else's unwelcome noise. So we buy some head phones and set about desensitising Liam. Their unfamiliar feel distresses Liam initially, but when he realises he can listen to his favourite music without incurring the wrath of others, he quickly settles into wearing them. He tries walking about with them on, dragging the tape recorder along with him. With more patient training he understands that to listen to music he has to sit still – no mean feat, but he is highly motivated and soon accepts the rules. Once these teething problems are overcome, Liam takes to listening to his music tapes with great enthusiasm. Every morning, as Liam comes bubbling and giggling into the classroom, instead of looking for somewhere to climb he makes his way to a quiet corner and happily plays and sings along to his favourite nursery rhyme tapes. He hasn't been given the opportunity to climb onto any worktops or surfaces and with such a satisfying replacement activity it is never a major issue for us.

On the rare occasions when Liam does try to climb (when he is bored or when we are distracted and he is restless) we deal with it in a quiet, unassuming manner. We approach Liam nonchalantly, giving nothing away about our displeasure or potential actions and then, before he can think that he might be doing something 'naughty', we lead him to some other activity with a calm indifference that gives nothing away. Our policy is to avoid, at all costs, saying 'No, Liam!' We have learned very early on that Liam just loves to be told off. His penchant for winding people up emerges as very much part of his personality. He seems to have an innate feeling for how and when to do something irritating to elicit a negative response. 'No, Liam!' is like music to his ears or a red-rag to a bull. In he charges, all cylinders firing, with doubled effort to do anything, just anything, to bring about that much loved word, 'No'.

Well, you are no doubt thinking, it's easy enough not to use the word. Well yes, it is easy, technically. Except that, if he can't elicit a 'no' then Liam is perfectly happy, and absolutely determined that he will drive you to at least have an exasperated 'no' tone to your voice. And it is surprisingly difficult to keep that tone out of your voice when responding to Liam's many deliberate acts of provocation! Liam knows, as we all do if we are honest, that it is impossible to hide an emotion if it is deeply felt or catches you by surprise. We discover the need for infinite patience and a calm, unruffled approach to life. This, of course, assumes a permanent level of super-human perfection on our part. We try, but Liam can be very persistent – and we are not super-human.

Here is an example of how persistent Liam can be. We are seated at the 'round table'. Nothing major has happened all day and this story-session will be a low-key affair. The routine is well established, so no one has to feel anxious about new challenges or potential failure. The session is familiar, comfortable and enjoyable. Having got everyone seated, the heat of the afternoon has lulled us all into a laid-back, can't really be bothered, mood. Alice crosses her arms on the tabletop and puts her head down, ready to listen to the story. Nathan is relaxed, Joss is flopped against Sally, and Lotti is slouched in her chair. Sam is half-asleep.

Toby and Liam sit side by side. There is nothing to unsettle the peace. The story quietly progresses. Liam decides to lean against Toby. Toby pushes Liam away. A little switch goes off in Liam's brain. He leans against Toby again, whilst at the same time giving Erin a broad grin of pure mischief.

'Sit up Liam.' In a neutral voice born of experience Erin smiles at Liam. He sits up. Triumphant, discreet smiles pass between me, Erin and Sally. We have been finding the quiet, neutral voice a great success in keeping Liam's mischief in check lately and here is another example of its efficacy. Did he sense our communal smugness? A few peaceful minutes pass. Thud! Liam's body lands against Toby, nearly catapulting him onto the floor. Toby, startled, cries out. Lotti sits up and growls. Alice lifts her head, glances nervously at Lotti, sees she is well out of striking distance and puts her head down. Erin, without ceremony, moves her chair between Liam and Toby, settles Toby and looks attentively at me, giving off the message 'Look everyone, Fran is telling a really interesting story and nothing else is going on'. Lotti, after a soothing stroke of her arm from Sally, slouches back down in her seat again. Toby sits alert but quiet.

I look gratefully at Erin and Sally. What a good team we have become, I think with satisfaction. Like a well-oiled machine, working silently but efficiently. I continue reading as if nothing has happened. Liam thuds into Erin. Erin pays no attention. He thuds into Erin again. She still refuses to respond.

Liam starts butting his head against Erin's shoulder. No response. Time for a new tactic. Twisting his head under Erin's chin, he looks up with his innocent blue eyes and, on failing to achieve eye contact, shouts 'Sit up Liam!' and grins. It is too much. The very faintest glimmer of a smile of amusement from Erin is all it takes.

'Hah! I've got 'em!' I don't think he said it aloud, but I'm sure we all knew at that moment that we had lost. Delighted with this sliver of a response, Liam continues, head still twisted upwards, eyes boring into Erin's face. 'Sit up, Liam! Hello Erin.' Erin shifts her weight so that Liam can no longer lean against her. He has to concentrate on not losing his balance. He regains his equilibrium and sits back up. Erin half-turns away from him. Liam settles back into his seat. I continue reading. It seems to have done the trick. No one else is disturbed, Liam has not managed to get himself chastised, Erin has contained her amusement and I am still reading. Ignoring Liam is a useful and successful strategy. And so easy.

Liam swings back in his chair. He starts to hum. Toby puts his fingers in his ears. Liam hums some more. Nathan, contentedly engrossed in the story, squeals angrily. Liam hums some more. In protest, Nathan squeals again and crouches up in his chair, ready to flee. Liam is delighted. He hums some more. Nathan, angry now, hits out at the nearest thing to vent his frustration. Unfortunately, the nearest thing is Alice. Alice, startled, lets out an almighty cry. 'He's killing me!' Toby reaches plaintively across to Sally for comfort. Lotti is disturbed and, distrusting the intentions of Sally's outstretched arm, takes a lump of flesh and gives it a meaningful pinch to register her displeasure. Joss, alerted by Liam's original cry, and tipped over the edge by Toby's sudden movement, joins the growing cacophony of hums, squeals, shouts and howls that have suddenly exploded into the hot classroom air. Erin turns angrily to Liam. 'No, Liam' – she very nearly admonishes!

Wind-up he may be, but he is utterly guileless too. As you can imagine we are not always aware when Liam is up to mischief, but he is very good at ensuring we don't miss any misdemeanour, however minor. 'Sorry Liam' and 'Kiss', spoken with his face turned upwards, eyes peering pointedly into my eyes and I know that Liam has done something he shouldn't. I know, but he apparently doesn't, that if he just kept quiet, he might get away with it. But he never does. Something in his open, sunny, mischievous personality compels him to not so much confess, but more to instantly apologise and thereby give himself away, every time. That is not to say that the apology is full of remorse and guilt. Rather, it is just what you do after you have done something wrong.

Way back in his short little life he has understood that he has to say sorry. He hasn't quite understood that you say it to the person you have upset. Or that you should at least sound as if you mean it. So he says sorry as soon as he has done something he feels he shouldn't – whether there is anyone around to hear it or not. And a kiss – well, that's to show there are no hard feelings. So simple, so innocent. So useful!

Liam's sense of humour and overwhelming goodwill towards us helps us all to tread this minefield that is his autistic world. His personality always shines through his difficulties and despite his infuriating ability to wind us up on almost every occasion his mischievous personality enhances our lives as much as I hope we, in the short time we worked with him, enhanced his.

Late one Friday morning, Liam's parents come into the classroom waving Liam's reading book and beaming proudly. Liam is late because he has been for his annual check-up with Dr M (his paediatrician). 'Liam read to Dr M. He couldn't believe that anyone with Liam's severity of autism is able to learn to read.' Following fast on the heels of a soulless Ofsted inspection, it is a wonderful endorsement of our efforts and our spirits lift. This is what makes our job so satisfying – not fitting into neat little boxes for government statistics.

Liam's parents have every right to be proud of their son. He has worked hard learning to read. He has had to rein in so many of his compulsions and repetitive behaviours and concentrate hard, something that does not come easy. Between us Liam and I have spent considerable time and effort cracking this particular educational challenge. For me, it has been another learning curve, where the problems of autism meet with the practice of teaching reading. It means unravelling those aspects of Liam's autism that can help him learn from those that are actively confusing the process. This involves being constantly on the alert. The fine balance between teaching what I think I am teaching, and Liam learning what he thinks he is learning, is often tipped against progress and towards confusion.

Reading is something we have done together as a shared activity on many occasions – both during group sessions and on a one to one basis. The next challenge is to teach him to recognise some key words. By tapping into his love of number Liam becomes a highly motivated learner. Once he realises that if he reads a word correctly, he keeps the card on which the word is written, he becomes very keen to collect more and more cards. His obsession with card collecting fuels his motivation to learn words. By the time Liam has learnt some key words by the flash card method he already has lots of knowledge about handling books and understanding how text works – i.e. text reads from left to right, follows from page to page and carries the story. So he is able to make good progress in transferring his new found skills in reading flash cards to reading books.

The difficulty, when it arises, creeps up on us both imperceptibly. He begins to encounter words in his reading books that he doesn't know. Every time he doesn't know a word, he looks away from the text and towards me, grinning broadly. He begins to slip into a habit of instantly looking away from a word as soon as he realises he does not know it. His reading becomes stilted, his focus changes and it seems that we are now playing some kind of game, whereby the whole point of reading, for Liam, is to get to a word you don't understand and then grin happily at the person sitting next to you. It becomes apparent that we have both lost the plot. What began as positive encouragement on my part has become the whole point of the exercise for Liam. Reading is fast losing all meaning.

It takes a lot of patient retraining on my part, learning that I must not take my eyes off the text, I must not look at Liam, I must keep a hundred per cent focused on the words on the page, I must become neutral, invisible almost, so that Liam does not get any mixed messages as a reader. For a while he continues desperately to try and gain eye contact with me every time he meets a word he does not know. He thrusts his head below mine bent earnestly over the book, and tries to get me to look at him, to tell him the word, to smile back. I have to persevere for some time, keeping my head bent, my concentration full on the text, my face a mask. Quietly, without lifting my eyes from the page I demonstrate using phonic skills. Sometimes I just say the word. (English is impossible to teach by phonics alone – it is not at all autistic friendly, rules-wise.) Gradually Liam realises that he can do as I do, and work out the words himself, by looking at the text, not at my face. Slowly, he gains confidence to try working out words and eventually he is back on track as a reader. To become a reader, Liam has not only had to learn skills, but he has also had to learn that he is central to the reading process.

As well as the day to day classroom learning, we regularly take the school bus and go into the wider community, to help to develop social skills and broaden horizons. One of our school outings is a trip on a miniature railway. It is a local venture, run by a group of enthusiasts. On this particular day an elderly gentleman and his young helper are in charge. We are their only passengers. Performing the appropriate role as enthusiastic teachers, we point out the job the young boy has of waving his flags at the driver. Liam develops the giggles. He is laughing at the young guard, who stands serious and erect and wholly engrossed in his duties as a flag waver. Liam is obsessively drawn to look at this boy and despite our best efforts at distracting him he is unable to take his eyes off him. He dissolves into ever more helpless giggles. He laughs so much he can barely get onto the train and practically falls off the seat, he is shaking so much with mirth. He is totally unfazed by his inappropriate social rudeness.

One of the more poignant aspects of autism that parents find particularly difficult in public is that their child looks like any other little five-year-old. There are no indications to the uninitiated that any bizarre or anti-social behaviour is anything more than the result of bad parenting, or a very spoilt child. Every parent has tales of judgemental members of the public tut- tutting at them disapprovingly as they struggle to drag a screaming child away from the video display at the local supermarket, or apologise when an unwanted food item in a cafe is thrown unceremoniously towards an unsuspecting granny.

'They look so normal' is both a blessing (no one would want to add physical problems to the enormous burden the disability already inflicts) and a curse, giving away no clues as to the disabling impairment their child is battling with. So there is something very poignant about Liam finding a young man, who had all the hallmarks of Down's Syndrome, the object of such merriment. On recounting the incident to his parents, they took it in their stride. They had had a similar experience when Liam, strapped in a supermarket trolley in a queue for the checkout, had spotted a young girl in a wheelchair and had an identical and similarly unstoppable laughing fit whilst his parents, like us, stood by, bemused and helpless to distract or control the inappropriate social embarrassment that is their sweet little son. As his mother explained, 'I could have died. Everyone is looking and you could tell they all thought he is a monster and we are monster parents too.' But, she added, with a truth born of experience, 'There's nothing you can do when he gets like that.'

Nothing indeed. Back at the train station, Liam is weaker still, laughter having turned his legs to jelly and his body to a floppy heap. Liam cannot settle himself into anything resembling a sensible state until the train, and the serious, dedicated, smartly uniformed guard, are completely out of sight.

Liam's giggling is an example of the often-inappropriate emotional responses that people with autism experience. In our class of seven, laughter covers a whole range of emotional states and responses. Alice sometimes laughs at a shared joke, such as when Liam puts his jumper on back-to-front. Sam does his best to share a joke. Ever anxious to please and conform, but not always understanding the context, he will make himself laugh if he thinks the social situation requires it of him. Nathan will often chuckle happily to himself in genuine amusement at some private joke. Lotti can fool you into thinking she is wonderfully happy, giggling away then inexplicably crossing over into tears without a moment's warning. Joss's giggle is often a useful early warning system, precluding mischief. For Liam, laughter seems to be very closely associated with embarrassment and anxiety.

Extreme nervousness can trigger an hysterical response in anyone, particularly in the moments before a hair-raising challenge. If you stand in any queue for the 'ultimate thrill' ride at a fair the chatter ranges from the bravado boasting of the confident, to the quiet anxiety of the terrified via the hysterical, forced laughter of those trying to both mask their fear and psyche themselves up for the challenge. Perhaps something of these emotions, drawn large, are playing upon Liam the first time he goes horse riding.

A line of children waits in anticipation as the horses are led out. Alice, Lotti and Toby all love horse riding. Sam is waiting rather anxiously, holding tightly to the hand of his assistant and trying hard to be brave. Joss is wildly, jumpingly, springingly excited. Nathan is cross and impatient – waiting is not his forte. And Liam is dissolving into 'that laugh' – the laugh he gets when he is about to become hysterical. The laugh that makes him go all floppy and legless. The unstoppable laugh. Oh dear, this is going to be a challenge.

Helping little five-year-olds, who are not the best at following verbal instructions, to mount a horse can be a slow and difficult job. Legs don't always go the way you want them to, knees often bend too soon or too late to facilitate an easy settling into the saddle, balance is not always maintained as feet are placed into stirrups, and the reins are not always taken up with a firm and confident grasp. For each child at the Riding for the Disabled session three adults are needed. One to lead the horse and keep it steady and calm and one on either side of the child to help them onto the horse and be ready to catch them, should the child suddenly decide he or she has had enough. But three adults is a hopelessly inadequate number when the boy who is being helped is literally creased up with laughter.

One thing I haven't yet mentioned about Liam and his laughter – this particular, hysterical, over-the-top unstoppable laughter – is that the more he laughs the more hypersensitive he becomes to touch. Touch exacerbates the whole giggling-falling-about-going-floppy scenario. For us, it always leads to a dilemma – yes, another one! (It is not possible to teach children with autism unless you have a confident line in dilemma solving!) In this case it is the dilemma of how to help Liam onto the horse – the unavoidable touching bit – and then back off so his hypersensitive giggle-trigger can calm down enough for Liam to regain some spine strength and sit up properly.

Once we get Liam on the horse he just flops forward, red-faced cheeks hitting against the patient horse's flanks as he chuckles away uncontrollably. We clutch grimly at his precariously floppy body, preventing him from literally laughing himself off the horse. Talking to him sharply, gently, imploringly, sternly, all are to no avail, as all the time it is necessary to keep tight hold of him, thereby continuing the now frustratingly annoying laughter. It seems that the cycle of laughter, floppiness, physical support, more laughter will never be broken and that Liam will have to be lifted off to watch from the sidelines, his first attempt at horse-riding being written off as a defeat.

But defeat is not something we do, at least not without exhausting all the possibilities. The only way forward is to try and break the cycle. We try a fresh start. We take him off the horse; stand him back in line and without responding to him beyond holding his hand we patiently wait for him to calm down. Then we approach the mounting block. But it is hopeless. As soon as he realises he is going back on the horse he once again dissolves into the kind of laughter that is dangerously contagious. After the third attempt, which leaves Liam, shoulders shaking with mirth, lying prostrate along the length of the horse's back, we decide it is make or break time.

For children with autism, making the initial leap from non-participant to participant in a new activity is a huge hurdle. Once overcome, a new world of experiences may open up for the child whose natural inclination is to spurn anything that is unfamiliar or unpredictable. If that initial leap is not made first time, then that reluctance can become an almost immovable obstacle in itself and can be such an entrenched part of the ritual of approaching that activity that the opportunity is forever lost. We therefore do all we can to ensure that new experiences are made as comfortable and as pleasurable as we can so that the child's horizons are broadened and experiences open up. If we had just given up on Liam on this first session, it may have been forever closed to him.

With this in mind, it is imperative that we find a way to move Liam beyond this uncontrolled laughter that is sabotaging his ability to access this new activity. The only way I can see to do this is to shock him into having to take control of his own actions. Surprise is what we need. Subvert his expectations that we will continue to hold him and he can continue to laugh. If we can force Liam to take responsibility for himself he might calm down and be able to stay on the horse. With a couple more adults for extra safety, and with a degree of reckless caution, it is decided that if this is not going to be a lost cause, then the only course of action left to us is to start the horse and leave Liam to come to his senses; to grab the reins and settle down; or to admit defeat as he falls off into the anxious arms of the nervously hovering adults.

Everyone lines up. Liam is helped back onto the horse. He continues his pattern of laughter and collapse. Quietly and calmly we tell him what is about to happen. The reins are placed where he can easily grab them. The horse is told to 'walk on'. Liam sobers immediately. He sits bolt upright and shakily, gratefully, grabs the reins. As he quickly (of necessity and in utter surprise) takes up the reins and feels the unfamiliar bouncing in the saddle as the horse plods on he grins. From then on he does what you would expect any five-year-old boy who has never been on a horse before to do. He sits bolt upright, holds the reins tight and adjusts, somewhat startled, to the wholly new sensation of horse riding!

Back in the classroom Liam, more than anyone else in the class, is responsible for what is known in the trade as 'the domino effect'. This is where the delicate balance of a class of children with autism can be tipped from calm to chaos. Generally, it will be started by one child feeling particularly out of sorts. His or her reaction then triggers someone else to get upset and so on. Usually it is possible to stop the chain of events from affecting everyone by well-timed intervention, but sometimes it happens. Everyone gets upset. The dominos fall. In our class when this happens it is usually Liam who is the trigger. To be fair, it occurs when more than one child has been out of sorts at some time during the day, or when there has been a particularly unsettling time. But Liam is often there at the beginning, stirring things up.

If Liam is bored, frustrated or cross he will do something to draw attention to himself. The most effective way of doing this is to up-skittle another member of the class. Knowing his hum, at a certain resonance, can drive poor Toby demented he might try this. If he can't get the pitch right, he might try wobbling sideways against Joss, breaking through his invisible 'keep out' sign and gate-crashing into his carefully guarded space. Or he might put his face right up against Nathan's and shout 'Hello' to Nathan, in that over-friendly manner that sends Nathan into paroxysms of anger. That is pretty much a dead-cert to elicit a response, but if Nathan is unavailable to torment, Lotti might be stirred into action. Liam will shuffle his chair at just such an angle as to spoil the symmetry of angles of chair leg to table leg perfection that Lotti has spent the last five minutes arranging, causing her to gnash and snarl threateningly. Failing all else, Alice is worth a try. With the wind in the right direction the usually calm Alice can be wound up into drama-queen mode. By hugging her he might be lucky and elicit a blood-curdling scream, 'Liam is breaking my arms!'

A startled Lotti will instinctively pinch the nearest unsuspecting victim, whose cries of pain and hurt will unsettle Joss. After sitting silent and stony faced for as long as possible Joss will begin to shed large, silent tears and gradually dissolve into deep hiccupping helpless sobs. Toby will notice this and join in the crying, his snot mingling with tears. In an overwhelming urge to launch himself at anyone for consolation he will upset Nathan. Fearful of any impeding dangerous contact Nathan will leap off his chair, causing it to crash to the floor. Sam, peace-loving Sam, will look on in dismay and begin to cry, pleading for it all to stop. Liam, of course, will be looking on and laughing! But then, the chaotic falling apart of any semblance of classroom order will begin to unsettle even Liam. He too joins in the shouting and tears. He starts to tell himself off, his loud 'No Liam' interspersed with lurches across the table in an haphazard attempt to reprimand all the others for getting into such a loud, unhappy, angry, frustrated, confused, unruly state.

We are in the helpless grip of the domino effect. Although you can see it coming, once it reaches a particular momentum you are helpless to stop it. Three adults are trying frantically to placate first one then another child, but three adults are pretty much helpless in the face of seven upset children with autism, each needing very individual and delicate handling. One by one order is restored and a fragile class settles back down again to its delicately balanced peace and harmony.

It doesn't happen often. Generally we are able to contain the total fall-out from the domino effect by a process of well-timed damage limitation. This is where we are successfully able to remove a link in the growing knock-on effect of upset causing upset. By calm, quiet intervention with an unaffected child, caught early, the whole edifice can be saved from crumbling. But if it is a day when two or more children are feeling particularly vulnerable and a hapless third gets caught up in the crossfire, there just aren't enough of us to intervene successfully. Then, like a forest fire ignited by the smallest spark, the domino effect takes hold, sweeps out of control and the whole classroom disintegrates.

And Liam is definitely our bright little spark!

Liam's parents talk about their son and what his autism means to them

Warren: I think we are very proud of him. Very, very proud. I think every day we are proud of him. I mean we were sat there tonight at tea-time nudging each other because he's only recently learned to do the squirty cream. It still makes us laugh, watching him do it. It's just such an achievement that we never thought he would do it. Simple things that most people take for granted, like opening a packet of crisps. I would say ten years ago, I would say I'd never see the day that he would open a packet of crisps. So when we sit down for tea and he's got jelly it is a bit of a giggle for us to watch him squirting cream on it. So, things like that, you do feel proud of him. I mean, I'm proud of both my boys but probably take [the younger son] a little bit more for granted, the way he's growing up, because I expect it I suppose of the progress he makes through life, but with Liam...

Laura: You see, every little thing he does, we don't expect. It's more of an achievement.

Warren: Yes, it's more of a milestone for him to have achieved it. So it does make you very proud... We've always accepted that Liam is autistic and always will be autistic. I think we've always been resigned to the fact, from day one, about what he is and who he is and we've never looked to any of these miracle cures. We've just said fine, if it works for them, brilliant, but we are quite happy with the young man that he is today and we were quite happy with the young child that he was at the time. We're quite happy with the man he's growing into. You see, we've always accepted Liam for who he is. We've never tried to put him on a pedestal and expect things that are out of his reach, so when he does do things it is an achievement and we do feel proud of the achievement he's made. Because, at the end of the day, his life is always going to be an uphill struggle, always. It's never going to be easy for him and we just love him for who he is basically. Don't we?

Laura: ...He's just Liam. We've also had this discussion with like other parents. We've said, 'What would you ever do if there was this cure, this 100 per cent cure where it was guaranteed to work on every child? Would you do it, go for it?' And we've said yes, I suppose you would, for Liam. We'd do it for Liam. You can't, like, hold him back purely because you want him to stay Liam, to stay the way he is now. But if he was cured, he wouldn't be Liam any more. You'd have to be getting to know your son all over again, like a totally different child if you know what I mean. He'd be like a stranger. He'd be a different person, you know. You'd do it though.

Warren: You'd do it for him. You'd give him that chance to be normal, to lead a normal life. But as Laura said, it would affect us harder than what it would him, because you'd lost a son that you've had all these years and you've got like a stranger to get to know. And he would be a stranger.

Laura: You used to get people saying, 'oh you mean Liam is like Rainman?'

Warren: They do get categorised by whatever the media is pushing out at the time. You get the autism awareness week and you get all these marvellous autistic savants creeping out of the woodwork. To put it bluntly, it's annoying. Because the first thing you get is 'Oh autistic! They're really clever aren't they?' You are like 'No!' 'You mean he can't count chopsticks thrown on the floor?'

         ... It's hard to explain to people what autism is. I mean, if Joe Bloggs off the street asked me what autism is now I would probably stumble, because all you can do is explain about your child, not about autism. You are explaining about your child. It's the only way you can do it. And you do try and get around it by saying – but there are other children and they do this – and adults. Because I always start mentioning that they do grow into adults, because people think autism is a childhood disability. They don't realise it's a lifelong disability. If you look in a dictionary it's described as childhood autism, but they do grow into adults... When they're younger, people obviously aren't aware. There's your boy, doing funny things and it's not always apparent they have special needs. I found, at the beginning, it was our parents that were the worse for it. 'Oh he'll be all right, he'll grow out of it.' I got sick of hearing that, in the first week, and obviously that was them being unable to accept they'd got a grandchild with a disability – both parents – which obviously at the time didn't help us...

It's apparent, yes, that there's something wrong with him, yes. But it's the arrogance and the ignorance of people. I don't think you ever get over the fact. It does annoy you. And we've never been embarrassed by how he is, or what he's like in public, because we accepted it from day one, you know, who he is and how he is. But when you get people staring and their jaws drop and they're like looking at you, you think, in this day and age especially people still don't accept that these individuals exist you know? And you still get the looks and you see them muttering, as if to say 'huh! They shouldn't be allowed out in public.' Terrible! They are just totally annoying. …He's just Liam. He's happy. Some of the more able autistic kids, you hear of them, don't you, and they know they're different. But I don't think Liam knows he's different. I sometimes think that he lives a blessed life, if you like. I mean there's so much corruption and hate, you know, and violence in the world and he's just totally unaware of it. He's in his own little world.

Laura: He's got his own little world, with people who love him, at home and at school. I mean, I know as teachers you're not supposed to get involved, but we know you do. And he goes to school and we know that from the minute he gets on the bus we know the helper on the bus has lovely feelings for him, and we know when he gets to school his teachers help him and have feelings for him and then of course he has the love that he gets at home and I think, it's not such a bad life after all you know…

Postscript

A Note to Educators

Policy makers and educationalists, take note. When asked to recall their overriding considerations when choosing an educational placement for their child with autism there was a unanimous concern that was expressed by all. Although a warm welcome, friendly staff, a pleasant environment and an educationally sound approach to teaching autism were some of the issues highlighted, everyone agreed on one overriding principle.

Joss's mum

"I just thought, I wanted somewhere that was safe. Safety was the first issue. I knew it had to be safe and I thought the Unit was safe. It's only when he did things that I realised he wasn't safe. So he's done things recently where they've had to make adjustments because of the way he's got out. So: safety."

Alice's mum

"I looked at another school…but it was mostly for normal children. It didn't have a fence round it. Children could just run from the playground into the housing estate, which was very frightening. They could go into the estate and be lost. The education – they said she'd be in a separate class from everybody else, there would only be about two or three of them – but it all come down to the fact that I didn't think it was a safe school. What put me to the Unit was that there was a big high fence around it and people watching the children all the time… I know some get over the fence now…but that was the main thing.

There was someone there to watch over Alice. She couldn't get out even if she wanted to."

Nathan's mum

"I didn't really know much about autism at that time. It was just the safety factor at that time, because at the time, if you let Nathan out he would run. He would run. He'd be off! So, at the time really it was just the safety factor."

Lotti's mum

"I was relieved [she went to the Unit] because they were on about taking her to a mainstream with a portakabin, but I said 'No way, as long as I'm breathing!' Because it wasn't secure enough. That was another one of my worries, because she didn't respect boundaries. I was scared to death she was going to hurt herself... So when I came in and seen the school – the doors were locked and the keys were up – I seen she was safe. And it took a few weeks to accept that she was safe there, and that if I'm not there, yes, someone else will watch her... Because if she gets out they're not going to watch her all the time with 30 other children too, but with small classes, there's three of you and six or seven other kids. You're going to you know if one's escaped... They didn't have to be chased because they would only have run into one of the other classes, that's as far as they could have got... That was a big issue for me because when she was in the mainstream nursery she used to get up and wander off... It wasn't structured for Lotti, it was structured for kids who accept boundaries."

Toby's parents (on visiting Forestpark)

"He was just everywhere, and the classes were just like, very open plan – one class to the next class. And the headmaster said straight away this isn't suitable for him. I mean, we knew it...to be honest with you, at that time all we wanted was somewhere where he was secure, because he was a runner. So we thought, it was nice and small and autistic specific, and the ratio of people in the classroom to child was very high, so it was virtually ideal."

Sam's parents

"...And really there was the issue of security, because at the time Sam was a runner. He would still run then. And not all the schools were locked, were they? I mean they went straight onto the dual carriageway and things at the back and a lot had no security…"

Liam's parents

"When we went to visit [another school] there was a Down's Syndrome girl, and she was obviously misbehaving, so they had put her – there was a curtain dividing the classroom and they had put her behind the curtain and said 'You sit there and think about what you've done' because she wouldn't put her socks on or something. But the naughty side of the classroom was where the door was. And we said if they put Liam on the other side of the curtain, where the door is, they'll come to collect him and he'll be gone! No locks on the door. And he'd be gone, out in the woods or somewhere. So straight away we knew it wouldn't be suitable… We just wanted something that was safe for him. A safe environment, where he would still be at the end of the day! He would have gone! But once we got him in there [to the Unit] we never looked back, did we?"

Appendix 1

Fun Books to Appeal to Your Child

Sharing a book with a child can be one of the most intimate and rewarding shared experiences with a child with autism. All the books below have been tried and tested and proved their worth as perennial favourites. Initially the reader has to do all the work, but in time the enjoyment becomes increasingly mutual. The excitement of seeing the unfolding of confidence, pleasure and shared fun with a child is very satisfying. The books are loosely divided into 'types' and the list is by no means exhaustive.

Books with lots of repetition and fun sound effects

These are great fun, and also good for anticipation, which encourages involvement at a variety of levels.

Campbell, Rod (1997) *Dear Zoo*. London: Campbell Books.
Inkpen, Mick (1999) *Lullabyhullaballoo!* London: Hodder Children's Books.
Inkpen, Mick (2000) *The Blue Balloon*. London: Hodder Children's Books.
Lavis, Steve (1996) *Cock-a-doodle-do*. Andover: Ragged Bears.
Martin, Bill and Carle, Eric (Illustrator) (1995) *Brown Bear, Brown Bear, What Do You See?* London: Picture Puffins.
Murphy, Jill (1995) *Peace At Last*. London: Macmillan's Children's Books.
Murphy, Mary (1997) *I Like it When*. London: Picture Mammoth.
Rosen, Michael and Oxenbury, Helen (Illustrator) (1997) *We're Going on a Bear Hunt*. London: Walker Books.
Ross, Tony (1986) *I Want My Potty*. London: Anderson Press.
Shigeo Watenabe (1991) *How Do I Put It On?* London: Red Fox.
Waddell, Martin and Barton, Jill (Illustrator) (1994) *The Pig in the Pond*. London: Walker Books.
Waddell, Martin and Oxenbury, Helen (Illustrator) (1996) *Farmer Duck*. London: Walker Books.

Books which are good for language pattern, singing, actions and rhythm

If you can get tapes to accompany these books, all the better.

Adams, Pam (Illustrator) *(1975) Old Macdonald had a Farm.* Swindon: Child's Play.
Beck, Ian and King, Karen (1998) *Oranges and Lemons.* Oxford: Oxford University Press.
Beck, Ian and Williams, Sarah (1991) *Round and Round the Garden.* Oxford: Oxford University Press.
Beck, Ian and Williams, Sarah (1991) *Pudding and Pie.* Oxford: Oxford University Press.
Brown, Mark (1987) *Hand Rhymes.* London: Picture Lions.
Freeman, Tina (Illustrator) (2001) *Ten Little Monkeys Jumping on the Bed.* Swindon: Child's Play.

Counting books

These are always popular – they are predictable, accessible and satisfying.

Carle, Eric (1994) *The Very Hungry Caterpillar.* London: Hamish Hamilton Children's Books.
Carle, Eric (2004) *1,2,3, To the Zoo.* London: Picture Puffins.
Hawkins, Colin (2003) *What's the Time Mr Wolf?* London: Egmont Books.
Inkpen, Mike (1987) *One Bear at Bedtime.* London: Hodder Children's Books.
Roffey, Maureen (1995) *Ten Little Teddy Bears.* London: Puffin Books.
Williams, Garth (1984) *The Chicken Book.* London: Picture Lions.

'Fact' books

Factual books appeal to children with autism. The most thumbed through in our book box were:

My First Look *At… series.* Dorling Kindersley

Sharing these books may be more challenging for the adult (at least if, like me, you like to build up the drama element of a story) but they are very satisfying for many children and again have the potential to encourage shared experience and shared pleasure.

Bunting, Jane (1999) *My First ABC.* London: Dorling Kindersley.
Machines at Work (2003) *Aeroplane.* London: Dorling Kindersley.
Machines at Work (2003) *Digger.* London: Dorling Kindersley.
Machines at Work (2003) *Fire Engine.* London: Dorling Kindersley.
Machines at Work (2003) *Tractor.* London: Dorling Kindersley.
Millard, Anne (1999) *My first Animal Book.* London: Dorling Kindersley.
My First Series (2002) *My First Word Book.* London: Dorling Kindersley.
My First Series (2003) *My First Number Book.* London: Dorling Kindersley.

References and Further Reading on Autism and Asperger's Syndrome

These recommendations are loosely organised under headings, but these headings are by no means exclusive. Any personal account about living with autism, for example, has implications in education. Similarly, help with behaviour can come from an insight gained in reading a personal account.

The two books on Asperger's have been included because they are wonderfully insightful books by young people. Although not about autism, and in many ways beyond the scope of experience of most of the children you read about in this book, they are nevertheless the sort of book every adult should read!

Personal accounts of living with autism

Blackman, L. (2001) *Lucy's Story: Autism and Other Adventures.* London: Jessica Kingsley Publishers.

Hughes, R. (2003) *Running with Walker: A Memoir.* London: Jessica Kingsley Publishers.

O'Neill, J. (1998) *Through the Eyes of Aliens: A Book about Autistic People.* London: Jessica Kingsley Publishers.

Overton, J. (2003) *Snapshots of Autism: A Family Album.* London: Jessica Kingsley Publishers.

Rankin, K. (2000) *Growing Up Severely Autistic.* London: Jessica Kingsley Publishers.

Schnieder, E. (2003) *Living the Good Life with Autism.* London: Jessica Kingsley Publishers.

Shaw, J. (2002) *I'm Not Naughty – I'm Autistic: Jodi's Journey.* London: Jessica Kingsley Publishers.

Sicile-Kira, C. (2003) *Autism Spectrum Disorders: The Complete Guide.* London: Vemillion.

Stone, F. (2004) *Autism – The Eighth Colour of the Rainbow: Learn to Speak Autistic.* London: Jessica Kingsley Publishers.

Williams, D. (2002) *Exposure Anxiety – The Invisible Cage: An Exploration of Self-Protection Responses in the Autism Spectrum and Beyond.* London: Jessica Kingsley Publishers.

Williams, D. (2004) *Everyday Heaven: Journeys Beyond the Stereotypes of Autism.* London: Jessica Kingsley Publishers.

Behaviour issues

Attwood, T. (2002) *Why Does Chris Do That?* London: National Autistic Society.
Clements, J. and Zankowska, E. (2000) *Behavioural Concerns and Autistic Spectrum Disorders: Explanations and Strategies for Change.* London: Jessica Kingsley Publishers.

Education related

Aud Sonders, S. (2002) *Giggle Time – Establishing the Social Connection: A Program to Develop the Communication Skills of Children with Autism.* London: Jessica Kingsley Publishers.
Beyer, J. and Gammeltoft, L. (2000) *Autism and Play.* London: Jessica Kingsley Publishers.
Lawson, W. (2001) *Understanding and Working with the Spectrum of Autism: An Insider's View.* London: Jessica Kingsley Publishers.
Moor, J. (2002) *Playing, Laughing and Learning with Children on the Autistic Spectrum: A Practical Resource of Play Ideas for Parents and Carers.* London: Jessica Kingsley Publishers.
Vermeulen, P. (2001) *Autistic Thinking: This is the Title.* London: Jessica Kingsley Publishers.
Waterhouse, S. (1999) *A Positive Approach to Autism.* London: Jessica Kingsley Publishers.
Williams, D. (1996) *Autism: An Inside–Out Approach.* London: Jessica Kingsley Publishers.

Practical guidance

Ives, M. and Munro, N. (2001) *Caring for a Child with Autism: A Practical Guide for Parents.* London: Jessica Kingsley Publishers.
Lawson, W. (2000) *Life Behind Glass: A Personal Account of Autism Spectrum Disorder.* London: Jessica Kingsley Publishers.
Legge, B. (2001) *Can't Eat, Won't Eat: Dietary Difficulties and Autistic Spectrum Disorders.* London: Jessica Kingsley Publishers.
National Autistic Society (2000) *Autism Handbook.* London: National Autistic Society.
Yapko, D. (2003) *Understanding Autism Spectrum Disorders: Frequently Asked Questions.* London: Jessica Kingsley Publishers.

Asperger's Syndrome

Jackson, L. (2002) *Freaks, Geeks and Asperger Syndrome.* London: Jessica Kingsley Publishers.
Sainsbury, C. (2000) *Martian in the Playground.* Bristol: Lucky Duck Publishing.

References

Claiborne Park, C. (1983) *The Siege.* Hutchinson Paperback.
Impey, R. (1972) *The Trouble with the Tucker Twins.* London: Viking.
Mesibov, G., Schopler, E. and Shea, V. (2004) *The TEACCH Approach to Working with People with Autism Spectrum Disorders.* Amsterdam: Kluwer Press.

Appendix 3

Organisations

A word of caution from Joss's mum:

"If you are a new parent you've got to think, 'Oh, there must be something, mustn't there?' You feel you must be able to do something and if you went on the internet you would just be bombarded with information and cures. It seems lately that the list just gets endless. I just say, you have to do your research very well before you embark on paying out lots of money, because we've been ripped off loads of times. But don't be afraid to try things."

The following recommendations are well-established organisations.

Autism Independent UK
119/201 Blanford Ave
Kettering
Northants NN16 9AT, UK
Tel/fax: 01536 523274

Autism Society of America
7910 Woodmont Avenue, Suite 300
Bethesda, MD 20814-3067, USA
Website: www.autism-society.org

British Institute of Learning Disabilities (BILD)
Campion House, Green Street
Kidderminster
Worcestershire DY10 1JL, UK
Tel: 01562 723010
Email: l.howells@bild.org.uk
Website: www.bild.org.uk

Dietary Interventions
Autism Research Unit
School of Health Sciences
University of Sunderland
Sunderland SE2 7EE, UK
Website: osiris.sunderland.ac.uk

National Autistic Society (NAS)
393 City Road
London EC1V 1NG, UK
Tel: 020 7833 2299
Email: nas@nas.org.uk
Website: www.nas.org.uk

National Autistic Society Scotland
Central Chambers, 109 Hope Street
Glasgow G2 6LL, UK
Tel: 0141 221 8090
Email: Scotland@nas.org.uk

National Autistic Society Wales
Glamorgan House, Monastery Road
Neath Abbey, SA10 7DH, UK
Tel: 01792 815915
Email: wales@nas.org.uk

Parents for the Early Intervention in Autistic Children (PEACH)
PO Box 10836
London SW14 9ZN, UK
Email: info@peach.org.uk
Website: www.peach.org.uk

Picture Exchange Communication System (PECS)
Pyramid Educational Consultants UK Ltd
Pavillion House, 6 Old Steine
Brighton BN1 1EJ, UK
Tel: 01273 609555
Email: Workshops@pecs.org.uk
Website: www.pecs.com

Treatment and Education of Autistic and Related Communication Handicapped (TEACCH)
Division TEACCH, School of Medicine
310 Medical School, Wing E 222H
Chapel Hill, NC 27514, USA
Website: www.teacch.com

Index